Business or Pleasures

Business or Pleasures

Free Enterprise;
-Africa's hope of an economic recovery.
-The determining factor of our financial future.
-Helping us to liberate our gifts, so that we all
succeed in business and life

Joseph Ager
Foreword By: Joshua A. Gana

iUniverse, Inc.
New York Lincoln Shanghai

Business or Pleasures
Free Enterprise;
-Africa's hope of an economic recovery.
-The determining factor of our financial future.
-Helping us to liberate our gifts, so that we all succeed in business and life

iUniverse books may be ordered through booksellers or by contacting:

iUniverse
2021 Pine Lake Road, Suite 100
Lincoln, NE 68512
www.iuniverse.com
1-800-Authors (1-800-288-4677)

ISBN-13: 978-0-595-40383-7 (pbk)
ISBN-13: 978-0-595-84758-7 (ebk)
ISBN-10: 0-595-40383-2 (pbk)
ISBN-10: 0-595-84758-7 (ebk)

Printed in the United States of America

Contents

FOREWORD

I and Joe have been learning from each other for a long time now and I'm glad at last we can share part of this wisdom with the world. I have known him since secondary education to confirm he is a man of purpose.

I strongly believe that free enterprise can lead to financial success for the individual, the community and the nation. This is a thought of the hour; in a world rapidly moving towards the free market place. Africa being left behind is a luxury we cannot afford, as this book presents the answers to the future.

Joseph Ager is one of the most inspirational individual I have known. We might not share the same politics but in this terrific piece of work, he examines what can really make all African governments work economically and indeed politically.

This is an inspiring book by one of free enterprise most astute advocate. But much more than just a defense of free enterprise, 'BUSINESS OR PLEASURES' sets forth sure principles by which we can meet the moral and financial challenge of the twenty-first century.

'BUSINESS OR PLEASURES' is full with stories and examples of people who simply refused to settle for anything. It draws you in and then reveals page by page that you too can be a success! He intentionally shows that circumstances will always try to limit you, but his emphasis lies in the fact that we are all overcomers. We possess such a vast amount of ability, and Joe aims to make us aware that anywhere and at anytime man has been free to act with these God-given talents, there are no limits to the things man can achieve. Above all, 'BUSINESS OR PLEASURES' is about people who have learned to believe in themselves and a God that does not fail.

While we read a lot of Western authors over the years try to define the "American dream", Joe is trying to make us all richer by showing us the way and calling us to build the "African dream."

This is the perfect book not just for the successful entrepreneur or the person who dreams of owning his or her own business. It is also for that sportsman or woman, artist, writer or musician. Joe makes it clear, we are all in business and love, purpose and pursuit are the keys to our success. Whatever you may need to succeed in business, above all learn love and passion. This book is a giant step in that direction.

'BUSINESS OR PLEASURES' is a must read for the aspiring entrepreneur as well as for those who have realized the personal successes of the free market system. Also, here, Joe tells you how you can make your dreams come true by centering your life in the love of God and country. Anyone who reads this book will have his or her outlook on time, work and money permanently changed. It is well written, consistently interesting, logical and persuasive. This book is for all people everywhere.

JOSHUA A. GANA
C.E.O.,
SUPERTEK NIGERIA LTD.

PRELUDE

This book will reveal to you that free enterprise has the answers for Africa's future. If we must get to our desired future, then free enterprise is the key system that will unlock that great future for us and our children's children.

Why is free enterprise the best economic system of the world and can't Nigeria and indeed Africa turn its economic fortunes around by embracing free enterprise? What is she holding back for? What are we scared of? All that is needed for us is to pay the initial price and in the very near future we will reap the fruits of our labour.

It is some what frustrating to know what you want but don't know how to get it. I personally believe that as we peep into the stories of wealth creation experts, you will be able to deduce that wealth flows in a particular direction—to the entrepreneur—maybe it's because they are bold enough to take certain risk, have special business acumen or have the ability for precision labour. Whatever it may be the list of this men and women is numerous.

It's also my believe that innovation is not limited to some few hot spots, but it is fast becoming an integral part of Africans identity. For sure, our struggles for success will face stiff opposition from some of world's elite and established entrepreneurs; we too could have a shoot at becoming household names in the future.

All I think we need is bold thinking, ability to work and the right kind of mentality to back a global vision.

'Business or Pleasure' might as well stir up in you that momentary spur to action. Howbeit, if you are careful, it could give you that motivation that will last you a lifetime and make you also a world's elite. Remember nothing stops commitment.

I have tried to blend the circular business principles with those that Jesus Christ encourages us to learn. The logic contained in this book as it's origin from God's success principle as contained in the Bible. These ideals can for sure give you an extra edge over any of your oppositions once you venture into the business world. There is great wealth waiting for you there. Read them, chew them, digest them—they are capable of making any one financially fat. Become a financial giant for yourself, for God and for your future generation.

Life on its own is a business. Since life is business, you will have need of a business mind. By studying the lives of those who have gone ahead of us, we could develop our own business acumen and rule the world with it too. I call those great folks, the 'business master minds'.

OVERVIEW

The story should be told that, at the start of the 21st century, you were indeed itching for an industrial revolution in your darling country. You viewed your future, your goals and plans; you wanted to do something with your life. And maybe during you brain storming, you decided that you would start up a business that would have a world—wide impact. In doing so, you taught about which common denominator you could choose if you were to affect lots of lives with the limits of your resources? If this piece of gist tickled you, then you could be on your way of condensing to a brilliant idea. As we will see from the lives and secrets of successful entrepreneur as well as some hard-core Bible truth, man is only able to achieve meaningful works in a free society.

As it been your life's dream to be in business for yourself? Because that's the reason why you picked this book. We understand that good success in today's fast-paced and ever-changing world can't be left to chance. If we want to be successful people, we must make a conscious effort to actively seek new ideas, innovations and growth. It is my sincere prayers that God will help us as we take this bold step and start businesses we've been dreaming about.

Our aim is that more and more young people in African countries will make it their vision and start building companies of their own. That they will make it their life's mission of creating exceptional products and services. Passion for their products along with the prospect of meeting a market need in our community should be their most critical motivator. Also, still if you want to prosper and help as many people as you possibly can to also prosper even in time of general economic hardship, then you should make it a life goal, to build your own enterprise. This is important because you have a right to be rich if you so chose to. It simply means to be fruitful, multiplying, subduing and having dominion. It means having enough money at any time to meet all your basic needs for food, housing, clothing, school fees etc. plus meeting the needs of those who depend on you for survival and still be left with a surplus to help others around you. Your goal should be simple; having an endless and ever increasing flow of income.

You have to achieve your mission in life because if you don't live up to your responsibilities, you will become a liability to your society. And I don't think you'll like to be a liability to your world. Failure is not an option in this journey of life. We must fulfill our destines and those of others. To do that, we must continually 'TAKE ACTION', live with passion, pursue our best and highest goals with determination, integrity, faith and a profound sense of living our life's mission.

This of course is a wake-up call to all sound minded individuals on this part of the world, that the free enterprise system or capitalism as you may call it—that worked for America and all other developed nations of the world—can also work for us. We too can establish a high profile in the worlds market and get ahead with building businesses that will receive recognition from elite entrepreneurs in other parts of the world. As Nigeria and Africa hopes to join the community of industrialized nations, individually, we should be delivering the future. We should aim to become the predominant multiple platform in the market. If your focus is unclustered, you should be able to combine a network of business and ideas that will have a multiple play strategy to offer consumers with the right thing, at the right time, on the right place as you evolve and establish your dream.

"THE MOST PATHETIC PERSON IN THE WORLD IS SOMEONE WHO HAS SIGHT BUT HAS NO VISION"

—Helen Keller.

1

NIGERIA
'A SURVEY'

UNDER THIS MANAGEMENT

"AS NIGERIAN'S PRESIDENT OBASANJO NEARS THE END OF HIS EIGHT YEARS. HE HAS MADE A GOOD ON HIS PROMISES OF REPAIRING THE DAMAGE DONE BY HIS PREDECESSORS. BUT THERE IS STILL A MOUNTAINOUS TASK AHEAD OF HIM AND HIS SUCCESSORS".

"The trouble with Nigeria is simply and squarely a failure of leadership. There is nothing basically wrong with the Nigerian character. There is nothing wrong with the Nigerian land or climate or water or air or anything else. The Nigerian problem is the unwillingness or inability of its leaders to rise to the responsibility, to the challenge of personal example which are the hallmarks of true leadership."

So wrote Chinua Achebe, the Nigerian novelist, in 1983. Between then and now, his gloomy book "The Trouble with Nigeria", has been perhaps the best short account available of how our country worked—or rather, how it did not work. Before president Obasanjo assumed office, Nigeria has been ruled by soldiers for all but six years since 1966. She has suffered one civil war, six violent changes of government, and the continual theft and squandering of public funds by its leaders. Blessed with fertile soil, floods of oil, and a huge, energetic, talented population, Nigeria should be Africa's giant. That it is instead one of the poorest countries in the world is largely the fault of a succession of awful military dictators. But with the return, perhaps of democracy, it has given Nigeria a chance to recover.

In 1999, general Abdulsalami Abubakar leader of the government then promised to restore democracy in stages with elections first for local governments, then for state governments, then for a national assembly and for the presidency itself. To many people's surprise, he kept his word. The election were marred by bribery of which parties were guilty—but the result is widely agreed to reflect the will of the Nigerian people. And on May 29th 1999, Olusegun Obasanjo, a 62-year-old chicken farmer, was sworn in as Nigeria's First Democratically elected president since the toppling of Shehu Shagari in 1983.

The challenge facing President Obasanjo than and even now is daunting. His country is poor, indebted and riven by ethnic violence (Which has left hundreds and thousands dead). The roads are pitted with potholes and logged with rubbish. Water and power lines work intermittently at best, and often not at all. Factories are idle. So, resentfully, are millions of urban youths. After a long spell of crude despotism, Nigeria has no tradition of democracy, nor of effective governance. For as long as most Nigerians can remember, the rewards for honesty and industry have been miserable, whereas corruption has paid magnificently Nigeria has become "the open score of a continent", in the words of Wole Soyinka, the country's 1986 Nobel laureate for literature.

WANTED: TRUE LEADERSHIP

Over five years after assuming power, president Obasanjo is still hard at work applying ointment to that sore. He has some useful qualification. First, although he was once Nigeria's military ruler, he was not personally corrupt, and had landed the top job more by chance than by plan. In 1976, after the assassination of the then ruler Murtala Mohammed, President Obasanjo, as his deputy took over. He stayed in office long enough to organize elections, and in 1979 handed over power to an elected civilian. It was not president Obasanjo's fault that the civilian regime was corrupt and was soon swept away in a coup.

So far, he has a mandate to keep Nigeria democratic this time. To this end, at the start of his government, he subdued the military, more than 100 officers with links to the old regime were retired, and non-political soldiers were put in—charge of the armed force. Some of those close to General Sani Abacha the last of the military dictators who died of a heart attack in June 1988—including his son, are being prosecuted for an array of alleged crimes, including murder. Efforts to recover some of the money the late dictator and his cronies stole have produced a haul of over $700m. There may be more to come.

Ordinary Nigerians, fed up with being robbed and bullied by their leaders, would probably like to see more harsh punishment for all old looters, but president Obasanjo, a former Political prisoner himself (he served three years of a 15 years sentence for allegedly plotting a coup against Abacha before the tyrant's death set him free), is inclined to be gentle. Indeed, Nigeria today is a far less fearful place than it was a couple of years ago. Good signs emerged when General Abubakar began the good work by releasing political prisoners and stopping security forces from harassing dissidents. Ever since then, president Obasanjo has continued in that vein (although his use of the army to crack down on some few trouble spots like in Rivers, Benue and Nigeria Delta has caused concern). Journalists at Nigerians dozens of lively, opinionated newspapers, who once risked being roughed up or worse by the security forces, now work unmolested.

On the economy, too, president Obasanjo has made a reasonable score. He claims to have abandoned the static philosophy he espoused in the 1970s and to have embraced the market. He did relax exchange control and promise to privatize, deregulate and fight corruption. For the first time in decades, there is a feeling of optimism in the air. Now that the country is no longer a pariah, America and Europe have sent in more aid. There is talk of debt relief of about $20billion already announced which is one of the pillars of success of this Administration, and perhaps even a good chunk of foreign investment. For the Nigerian in the street, the most visible change is the easy availability of petrol. Under past regimes, pumps ran dry and our leaders together with their friends made fortunes cornering supplies at the low official price and settling them at the much higher black market rate. Daylong queues formed outside petrol stations. For the citizens of one of the world's largest oil-producing countries, not able to buy fuel was perhaps the worst humiliation. President Obasanjo all but ended it with a few honest appointments.

President Obasanjo comes closer than any of Nigeria recent presidents to proving the "true leadership" Mr. Achebe called for. But his predecessors left Nigeria so horribly broken that it will take a lot of time and skill to mend it.

THE LAST DESPOT

In 1994, Wole Soyinka predicted that Sani Abacha would be Nigeria's last despot. Mr. Soyinka argued, that after his passing Nigerians would never again submit to military rule. With luck, he may be proved right. The army got such a bad name and hardly anyone in Nigeria now has a good word to say for the men in green. The most political generals have been sacked. These who are not being prosecuted have retired to their estates to play with their

Lamborghinis. Doubless this leaves behind some ambitious junior officers who still hope one day to make their own fortunes in government. They may be biding their time, waiting for a suitable opportunity for coup. Ethnic violence or an economic collapse might one day provide such a pretext. But for now, democracy is popular. Our military rulers parting gift to the nation they pillaged was to make Nigerians determined never to see their like again.

Most of Nigeria's uninformed rulers have been heavy-handed. When General Muhammadu Buhari seized power in 1983, he decided that military rule discipline was the way to put Nigeria to rights. His thugs started enforcing orderly queuing and the flying of the national flag above every shop, from department stores to roadside fruit stalls. On the last Saturday of every month, all Nigerians had to stay home and clean up their neighbourhoods. Civil servants who arrived late for work were force to do the "frog-jump", leaping up and own in a squatting position with their hands on their ears. Some suffered heart attacks. General Ibrahim Babangida, who overthrew Buhari in 1985, was more crafty in his exercise of power, but more ruthless too. In 1990, he had 69 fellow army officers executed after trails before a military tribunal, for allegedly plotting a coup against him.

Abacha who took over in 1993, brought Nigeria to new lows. Dissidents were beaten, hung upside down and starved to make them confess or implicate others. Political prisoners where tried in camera before martial courts that rarely set them free. Common criminals, such as armed robbers, were whisked through swift summary courts and shot without the right to appeal. In 1995, Abacha had the novelist Ken Saro-wiwa hanged even as leaders of the British commonwealth, gathered in New Zealand for a summit, were trying to persuade him to show mercy. Nigeria was expelled from the commonwealth the next day, and limp sanctions were imposed on it.

Abacha persecuted many of Nigeria's most famous offspring. Olusegun Obasanjo, the current president, was jailed after a rigged trail for treason. Shehu Yar'Adua who are President Obasanjo's deputy in the 1970s, died in custody in 1997, some say of a lethal injection administered by Abacha's hired killers. Moshood Abiola, a millionaire businessman who was set to win the 1993 presidential election before the army cancelled the vote count, was jailed for declaring himself president. When he died in jail within a month of Abacha's death, apparently of heart attack, some of his fellow tribesmen assumed that he had been murdered to prevent a Yoruba winning power. Many people died in the ensuring riots. In 1994, Abacha had Mr. Soyinka's Nigerian passport confiscated, driving the writer into exile in America where many members of the Nigerian middle class had already emigrated in search of easier life.

When Abacha died, the terror ceased. Abdulsalami Abubakar, the interim ruler, gradually released some 140 political prisoners and oversaw the free and reasonably fair elections that elevated Mr. Obasanjo to the presidency. Then, military budget was cut. President Obasanjo hopes that the UN will continue to help pay for Nigeria's peacekeeping efforts in sierra Leone, Liberia and other African war spots, which have cost an estimate of $10 billion over the past decade. Abacha's son Mohammed and four others still facing trial for the murder of Abiola's Wife, Kudirat, in 1996. An investigation into past human rights abuses, loosely modeled on south Africa's truth commission tried over 11,000 submissions. There are still reports of police an army brutality, but overall the state is incomparably more respectful of human rights than it was. Some Nigerians lament that the newly restrained police are not tough enough on thieves and hijackers. But most celebrate the death of despotism, and hope that it never revives.

A TALE OF TWO GIANTS
WHY INDONESIA HAS BEATEN NIGERIA HANDS DOWN

To understand the scale of Nigeria's future, it is helpful to compare it with Indonesia. The two countries are superficially similar. Both are huge, populous (Indonesia has 200m people; Nigeria perhaps 120m), and ethnically diverse. Both countries have suffered military rule and, at times, terrible violence. At independence in 1945 and 1960 respectively, both Indonesia and Nigeria were extremely poor; most of their people were subsistence farmers. But then both struck oil, and after the sudden quadrupling of the oil price in 1973-74 both were deluged with flood of petrodollars.

Nigeria has received some $300 billion in oil revenue since the early 1970s. Through foolish investment, graft and simple theft, this vast fortune has been wholly squandered. In fact, because successive Nigerian governments borrowed billions against future oil revenues and wasted that money too, it is fair to say that Nigeria blew more than its entire oil windfall. Nigeria despite the recent surge in the oil price, and the country is saddled with debts of about $30 billion. Income per head in 1998 was a wretched $345 less than a third its level at the height of the boom in 1980. For 2004, it is a little much better.

Indonesia, which has not always been a model of good governance either, has fared much better. GDP per head rose from under $200 in 1974 to over $1,000 in 1996 and 1997.

A currency crash brought it tumbling down to below $500 in 1998, but it bounced back to an estimated $700 last year. Indonesia's cake not only grew fast; it was also, despite the depredations of the Sahurto family, more fairly sliced than Nigeria's shrinking one. In the mid—1990s, the poorest fifth of Indonesia's people accounted for 8% of national income, compared with about 4% for the bottom fifth in Nigeria. By 1997, according to the United Nations Development Programme (UNDP), Nigerians were more than twice as likely as Indonesia's to be illiterate or to die before the age of 40, and seven times as likely to lack access to basic health care.

What could account for such disparities? Corruption was undoubtedly a factor. Bad in Indonesian, it was much worse in Nigeria. Raconteurs in Lagos bars tell it this way; "A Nigerian and an Indonesian attend a foreign university together in 1960s and become friends. After graduation, each returns home to join the government. Several years later, the Nigerian visits his colleague in Jakarta, and finds him living in a big, Luxurious house with a Mercedes car parked outside. 'How can you afford such a nice house on a politician's salary?' asks the Nigeria. 'Do you see that road?', replies the Indonesian, pointing to a magnificent highway outside. Ten percent. Some time later, the Indonesian goes to visit his Nigerian friend, and finds him living in a vast palace and with ten Mercedes cars parked outside. Amazed, he asks where the money had come from. 'Do you see that road?' asks the Nigerian, pointing to a thick tangle of rain forest. 'A hundred percent.'

A recent World Bank study puts t more soberly; Indonesia turned oil income into productive investments, whereas Nigerian oil income was either siphoned abroad or used for prestige projects."

The oil money came so suddenly, and in such vast quantities, that the government did not know what to do with it. In 1960, oil accounted for 1% of federal government revenues. Since then it has risen to about 95%. It was easy money. Foreign firms found and extracted the oil; the Nigerian government simple opened its coffers and watched the dollars gush in. The generals, assuming that the boom would last forever, spent carelessly. They also helped themselves and their friends to a big wad of the cash.

Most of Nigeria's rulers have been crooked, but some have been probably more crooked than other. Whereas others usually made at last some efforts to disguise their thieving, for example by laundering the loot through dummy companies, some simply grabbed it straight from the treasury and stashed it in their offshore accounts. Most of the extra revenue from increase in fuel price, which ostensibly was supposed to be channel into infrastructure and other investments, become blatant scam. The funds were not independently audited, and almost none of the monies sloshed through were properly accounted for. It was easy way for our past leaders and their friends to spend at will a sum that is equivalent to United States federal budget. Some went on padded contracts for friends. Some was stolen. Our military leaders themselves, ever nervous of their position as unselected, unpopular leaders, spent lavishly on their personal security, and handed out bricks of banknotes to bigwigs whose support they wanted to buy.

THE FAT OF THE LAND

How much did Nigeria's military rulers steal for their own use? Newspapers in Lagos bandy about numbers in the tens of billions, but the true total will probably never be known to Kaduna visitors where a number of retired generals live, cannot fail to be impressed by their huge mansions, complete with private mosques and satellite dishes bigger than many poor peoples houses, not to mention dozens of the sort of snazzy sports cars seen parked outside the Kaduna polo club.

But even more harmful to Nigeria that the generals' thieving was the way military governments squandered money they were legally entitled to spend. If not until when President Obasanjo came into office, visitors to the Ajaokuta steel plant, for instance, were surprised to see goats grazing among the gantries and children playing by the silent rolling mills. Nigeria flushed away a total of $8 billion trying to build a steel industry at Ajaokuta and elsewhere. The idea, first proposed in the 1970s, was that the country would become the Japan of Africa by industrializing heavily. Steel mills would turn local coke and iron ore into shiny metals, which would then be used to build railways. Contractor from the Soviet union, tendering to build Ajaokuta, produced 21—volume feasibility study, but it was never translated from Russian, and probably never read by any Nigerian decision-makers. They wanted a steel industry whatever the cost, partly as a matter of national pride, and partly because big projects brought big kickbacks. Ajaokuta has yet to produce a single bar of steel, as at the start of this present administration, and it will probably never be able to do so at a profit except it is privatized. Other steel mills in Nigeria operated fitfully, at a loss, and usually at a small fraction of capacity when the present government came on board.

Another example of how corruption bred waste in Nigeria is the cement scandal that broke under the civilian regime of Shehu Shagari in the early 1980s. President Shagari announced a grand public housing project, for which his government ordered vast quantities of cement—more, it turned out, than Nigeria's ramshackle ports could cope with. Ships loaded with cement formed a queue stretching for miles outside Lagos harbour, creating a spectacle that commercial pilots would take a detour to gawp at and racking up months of demurrage fees. Meanwhile the officials responsible were making a fortune from selling cement import licenses.

Perhaps the most egregious example of pointless extravagance is the capital city itself. Abuja was conceived as a symbol of national unity, a new capital at the center of the country, unburdened by connections with any of Nigeria's many squabbling ethnic groups. Instead, it became a symbol of the profligacy of the regime of general Ibrahim Babangida (1985—1993), which sank billions into the project and produced a glittering ghost town. No ordinary Nigerian can afford to live there, but no governor can afford not to make regular begging trips to the capital. Though Abuja is a picture to behold.

In the world corruption rankings compiled by Transparency international, a Berlin-based consultancy, Nigeria has consistently been among the worse offenders. Last year it was rated the second most crooked country, beaten only by Bangladesh. The pilfering continued right until the end of general Abubakar's transitional government. In the last months of military rule, a flurry of public contracts went to well—connected firms. Nigeria's foreign-exchange reserves shrank from $6.7 billion at the end of 1998 to $4 billion at the end of March 1999.

The new democratic government also have some explaining to do if at the end of their tenure they don't come up with why so much billions have been spent on the national I.D. card scheme and no result is visible. Though this government seems determined to clean up this mess somehow or other. But having sacked a few powerful thieves is not enough. The whole Nigerian political system, built up in a series of unfortunate steps over the past 40 years, built up in a series of unfortunate steps over the past 40 years, tends to encourage corruption. To curb it, president Obasanjo must change the system itself.

THE STONY ROAD TO REFORM
—SO MUCH TO DO, SO HARD TO DO IT—

For a crusader against corruption, president Obasanjo has fine credentials. When he was last in charge of the country (1976—1979), he kept his fingers out of the till. Until 1999, he was chairman of Transparency international's advisory council. Since assuming office, he has done many of the right things. Besides forcing crooks out of office, he was introduced the due process policy for awarding of contracts. He appointed more able and honest men to run public agencies such as the petroleum sector, and does not hesitate to launch a probe into every wrongdoing.

Only the biggest offenders will be prosecuted because punishing everyone who takes bribe would mean sacking virtually the entire civil service, thereby bring government to a standstill. What matters most is for people to know that from now on graft will no longer be tolerated. But moral admonitions will not be enough. It is traditional for Nigeria rulers to announce firm policies in the past and no single implementations taken.

So far, president Obasanjo's anti-corruption drive seems admirably non-vindictive, but to have chance of reducing corruption in Nigeria to tolerable level, two drastic changes needs to be done.

First, he must reduce the temptation to seek bribes by paying bureaucrats adequately. Secondly, he must loosen the states grip on the economy. This is not only desirable in itself, it will also reduce the power of officials to extort rents from Nigerian business.

Given the government's precarious finances, paying public servants adequately will not be easy. In the past, civil-service salaries were reviewed only occasionally. Typically, they would be lifted to a fairly generous level when the oil price went up and then frozen for several years, so that Nigeria's high inflation rapidly reduced them to les than a living wage, even if they managed to get paid. Civil servants had the choice of taking an extra job or treasuring bribes. Many chose bribes.

Lower-rung government employees are used to being paid late or not at all. Central-government revenues fluctuate wildly with the oil price. These fluctuations are reflected in the payments that trickle down to teachers, nurses and so on, and can be exacerbated if the officials in charge of disbursing their salaries are dishonest. Many states and local governments have been published audited accounts for years, so a lot of money seeps away as it passes through the system. This is one reason why so many schools and hospitals in Nigeria barely function. Unpaid staff are reluctant to show up for work. Those who do turn up often find that there is no budget for day-to-day running costs.

EXERCISE THE GHOSTS

One way to free up funds to pay civil servants properly would be to reduce their number, starting with the unknown but certainly huge number of "ghost" workers who get paid even though they are dead, or who never existed in the first place. Their salaries are pocketed either by relatives or by the officials who invented them. This kind of graft will be hard to curb until regular payroll records are kept.

To reduce the opportunities of corruption, fundamental changes will be needed to the way the Nigerian economy works. The instincts of the generals who have ruled Nigeria for most of the time since independence have been deregister. In the late 1960s and early 1970s they absorbed the ideas that were then fashionable: that governments of developing countries should seize the commanding heights of the economy, that the state should direct investment into "strategic" sectors such as heavy industry, and that all sorts of subsidies and controls were necessary to nurture and protect domestic agriculture and nascent manufacturers. Doubtless they sincerely believe all this. Their belief may have been reinforced, however, by the discovery that they could also direct money into their own pockets.

Contracts for building strategic factories were often parceled out among firms owned by members of the tender board. Controls imposed costs that businessmen were prepared to pay bribes to avoid. In Nigeria, getting a license to do more or less anything productive has for decades been conditional on handing over large amounts of cash. Subsidies were generally stolen before they reached their intended beneficiaries. Monopolies led to dreadful service and a tradition of demanding bribes to make it less. So, a few thousand naira to have a water line installed in days rather than years, a few thousand more to get power lines mended.

Past attempts at reform have failed, not least because so many Nigerians in top positions have benefited personally from bad policies. For example, in 1986, a year in which oil prices halved and Nigeria's finances accordingly fell into disarray, Ibrahim Babangida, the then ruler, tried to liberalize his way out of the mess. He adopted an IMF-style "Structural adjustment" programme which involved setting the exchange rate free, abolishing import licenses, slashing tariffs and removing most price controls. The programme failed, for two reasons. First, General Babangida was too preoccupied with political problems to follow through his reforms, and second, vested interests resisted any kind of liberalization. When one opportunity for graft was closed (Such as import licenses), officials created another, such as embezzling the governments windfall from devaluation. The fiscal deficit ballooned to almost 10% of GDP. Ordinary Nigerians agitated for democracy. General Babangida called an election in 1993, but annulled it soon after when Sani Abacha, his defense Minister, grabbed power, he re-imposed many controls on the economy.

Now, although the naira is not yet fully convertible, its rate is set daily at more or less market levels, and oil companies are allowed to sell dollars direct to anyone who wants to buy them. So the gulf between the official and black-market exchange rate has all but vanished, and with it the opportunity for arbitrage.

President Obasanjo has also ended the scam whereby officials deliberately created petroleum shortages to drive up the black—market price, thus enabling them to make a huge profit on reselling fuel bought at low official prices. The price at the pumps is still fixed by the government, but no longer at absurdly low levels.

The president professes to have embraced market economics, but he does no seem to have conquered his static instinct entirely. Though no petroleum minister or trust fund, but still President Obasanjo has a special adviser in charge of special projects." He seems to believe that corruption can be eliminated by appointing honest men. This is clearly a good idea, but so is the introduction of checks and balances that makes it harder to waste or steal public funds. Worryingly, president Obasanjo has promised to re-introduce fertilizer subsidies. He rightly points out that stimulating agriculture is the quickest way to raise large numbers of Nigerians out of poverty, and that lost of rich countries also subsidize farming. Yet when the fertilizer subsidy was swallowed by middlemen and fertilizer supplies became erratic because so much was smuggled abroad.

For Nigeria to recover, president Obasanjo must create a climate conducive to doing business. Neither foreigners nor Nigerians (Many of whom have a lot of money squirreled away abroad) will invest in Nigeria just because the president tells them that it is their moral duty to help rebuild a battered nation. The obvious place to start promoting investment is in the oil sector.

OIL ALONE DOESN'T MAKE YOU HAPPY
YOU ALSO HAVE TO KNOW HOW TO MANAGE IT

It happens almost every week. Youths burst into the offices of a foreign oil company, waving sticks and machetes and take a few employees hostage. Their demands: money for their community, and jobs for themselves, in any other part of the world, this would not be a good way of making a job application. But in the Niger Delta it sometimes works.

About 2m barrels of oil are pumped out of the delta's mangrove swamps every day, providing Nigeria with a variable but large chunk of its GDP, over 90% of its export earnings and almost all its tax revenue. Since the 1970s, the delta has generated hundreds of billions of dollars, but the people who live here have barely benefited. Despite all the energy, the region produces, many of them have no electricity. Their nights are lit only by the gas flares a top the oil rigs, which spew out pollutants that cause acid rain.

What the central government did not grab, local political stole or wasted, complaints addressed to the old regime often landed the complainants in jail, or worse when Ken Saro-wiwa, a writer and champion of the Ogonis, a small rivers tribe, was hanged in 1995, people got the message and took to raising their grievances direct with the oil companies.

The quickest way to capture an oil firms attention is through violence. Since President Obasanjo came to power, dozens of oil workers have been kidnapped. Most are released unharmed. The oil firms insist in public that they do not reward extortion. "The best security is to be welcomed by the local community, "insists, a spokesman for shell, the Angle-Dutch firm that handles about half Nigeria's oil production. But the truth is that kidnapping pays. Oil companies in the Nigeria delta spend million of dollars a year on community relations, on things like building schools and jetties in areas where they operate and compensating those whose land is polluted by spills. Locals have found that they are more likely to win a share of such goodies if they invade a rig or capture a company helicopter and that their claims for compensation are processed faster. Thugs who apply for jobs by brandishing machetes are sometimes put in the payroll. Often they draw wages but fail to show up for work. The oil companies prefer it that way' oil-drilling is a skill and not particularly labour intensive task, and having untrained people on site could be dangerous. Paying this kind of protection money is just one of the costs of doing business in the Delta.

President Obasanjo declared when he assumed office that solving the problems of the Niger delta would be one of his first priorities. A clause in the present constitution offers a guarantee that at least 13% of federal oil revenues will be returned to the state where the oil is produced, compared with 3% previously. President Obasanjo was hoping that this would kick-start development and gradually ease tensions. But calming this region is proving difficult.

The oil industry employs only about 100,000 people, so if the delta's wretched unemployment is to be reduced, other types of work will have to be found. Agriculture and fishing are the obvious traditional alternatives, but oil is bad for both of them. Leakage from ill-maintained pipes kills fish and renders arable land barren (oil and Agriculture don't mix). Since the compensation paid for ruined land often exceeds the likely returns from farming it, locals some times puncture the pipes themselves. Shell estimates some times back that, of 131 spills that year, 51 were caused by sabotage. Vandalizing pipes carrying inflammable liquid is hazardous. In one incident we won't forget in a rush in 1998, about 1,000 people were burned to death as they scooped up free fuel from a large spill near the town of Jesse. But Nigeria doesn't have money to burn.

Throwing money at the Niger delta may actually aggravate tensions there, as rival ethnic groups fight each other to claim bigger portions of the new, ledger pie. To take one incident among many, about 50 people were killed in November 1999 when members of the Oleh and Olomoro tribes squabbled over some water pipes that shell was trying to donate to their communities.

In 1998, violence in the delta escalated after the "two-million-man march", when Sani Abacha, in an effort to buy a bit of legitimacy, bused people from around the country to Abuja and paid them to rally in favour of his rule. For youths from the Niger Delta who took part in this extravaganza, the sight of Nigeria's capital was a revelation. They goggled at the smooth roads, the gleaming hotel and the splendid houses that oil money had bought for their rulers. They noted that whereas the delta has thousands of rivers but almost no bridges. Abuja has hundreds of bridges but no rivers to speak of. They realized for the first time how badly they had been robbed, and have nursed an implacable sense of grievance ever since.

THE RICH GET RICHER

Oil firms have yet to see any real results from the money they have spent on community development. In the past their goodwill money was channeled largely through traditional tribal chiefs, and often went no further. "We'd give a village a boat to set up a ferry business and the chief would just grab it and use it as his personal transport", complains one oil executive. Ken Saro-wiwa was hanged because he was said to have had some of those crooked chiefs murdered. The trail was a charade and the writer died protecting his innocence, but the animosity between Saro-wiwa followers and traditional Ogoni Chiefs was real and often bloody.

Shell, which wants to ensure that the over $38 a year it hands over to secure local goodwill is well spent, recruited two dozen experts from development agencies to monitor its community programmes. But there is a limit to how much the multinationals can do without better government. At a recent meeting between shell representatives and a dozen local politician from delta states the deputy speaker of the rivers state assembly put his priorities as follows: "Shell must give us water and light. The Federal government must give us more money. Foreign investors must come. Then we will have development."

Against this turbulent background, president Obasanjo is determined to increase Nigeria's oil production from 2m to 4m barrels a day by 2010, and proven reserves from about 25 billion barrels. In the past, one of the blocks to the investment needed to meet these targets was the federal government itself. The government claims ownership of all Nigeria oil. Foreign oil firms must operate as minority partners in joint ventures with it. The foreigners bring most of the know-how; the government's only obligation is to shoulder its share of the investment. In the past, it often failed to pay up.

Under president Obasanjo, payments have been prompt, but lefty arrears remain. The present government is trying to find alternative forms of finance. This means that the oil companies will cover more of the up-front costs of exploration and drilling, and will in return receive a greater share of the profits. They also plan within this decade to stop wastefully burning off the natural gas that is found with the oil. Instead, this gas will be turned into fertilizer, or liquefied and sold as fuel. This rather obvious strategy was first mooted 30 years ago, but never implemented.

"The government is serious about oil," says a senior Nigerian director at shell. We are confident that things will get better." But doing business in the Niger delta will continue to be hair-raising for years to come. "Community disruptions", as shell calls them, have grown more frequent. In 1997 the firm suffered 106 such incidents, last year almost twice as many. Several times, president Obasanjo has seen troops into the delta to quell unrest. The violence regularly prevents oil firms from honouring commitments to buyers. And spare parts are hard to come by in a region which some foreign suppliers shun for fear of being kidnapped.

STRIVING AMID CHAOS
THE BIGGEST HEADACHE OF NIGERIAN
BUSINESS IS UNCERTAINTY

Oil firms have their own particular problems, but they share more general headaches with every other kind of business in Nigeria. The water taps rarely work. Electricity comes in "periodic vengeful surges…as if the god of lighting has…taken personal charge", as Wole Soyinka puts it. When the traffic police knock off for lunch, cars soon become so grid locked that crippled beggars in hand-propelled skateboards outpace the motorists on whose windows they imploringly tap. Getting to appointments on time is tricky. Reliable services are so hard to come by that firms barter contacts. We'll let you share the electricity from our generator if you can help us find spare parts for it.

Firms wanting to set up in Nigeria are faced with a problem known locally as "BYOI" (Bring your own infrastructure). Cadbury Nigeria, for instance, in the absence of reliable power or water suppliers, generates eight megawatts of its own electricity and drills 2,500 feet down to obtain the 70,000 gallons of water an hour it needs for its Lagos good-processing plant. Since the water spurts out at 80^{0}C, it has to be cooled before it can be used. According to the firms managing director, BYOI adds at least 25% to operating costs. Many Nigerian firms, particularly the state owned ones, devote little effort to maintaining their equipment, so it often breaks down capacity utilization in the manufacturing sector is a miserable 28%. Once when one European factor boss in Lagos, pestered by head office to draw up contingency plans for coping with the millennium bug, scoffed: "If everything breaks down, how will we notice the difference?

Fraud too is a big problem. For decades, honest toil has been less well rewarded in Nigeria than swiping public funds or swindling fellow citizens. Abroad, the country has become a byword for advance fee scams and drug peddling. But the biggest sufferers at the hands of Nigeria's ingenious criminals are the Nigerian themselves. Laden lorries disappear. Accounts remain unpaid. Subscriber to the awful national telephone operators, NITEL, Sometimes find their bills hugely swollen because their lines have been rented out at night to people who want to call their relatives in Europe and America.

Francis Fukuyama, an American Social Scientist, a few years ago wrote a book arguing that only societies, whose people trusted each other, and their institutions, would be able to compete successfully in the global economy. If he is right, then Nigeria is in trouble. Most Nigerian avoids paying taxes, not least because they assume their money will be filched. Businesses do not extend credit to customers, because they do not expect to get paid. Banks do not issue credit cards, and shops do not accept them. Personal cheques are out of question. Guests at plush hotels must pay in advance, in cash, not only for the room but also for any meals the manager thinks they may eat or telephone calls they may make. Foreigners paying with dollars must wait while each bank note is scanned to detect forgeries, and the serial number of each bill is painstakingly recorded to make sure the staff resists temptation.

Because Nigerians do not trust each other, they have to pay cash for more or less everything. Until recently the highest banknote was 50 naira (worth a mere 50 cents). This present government introduced 100naira, 200 and 500 naira, but even then counting out the cash for a restaurant bill can still take several minutes. Business travelers must carry around suitcases full of naira. Nigeria's banks have made so much money from foreign exchange arbitrage that few bother much with ordinary customers. Small time traders fear that business opportunities will disappear in the time it takes to make a withdrawal, so they keep their working capital stuffed under the bed. And the banknotes themselves, after so much handling, are dirty and smelly. A study by researchers at Lagos University found that 86% of them were infested with the sorts of microbes that cause diarrhea.

HOW TO WIN WITHOUT CHEATING

Doing business in Nigeria is difficult, but it is not impossible. That nothing works is both an obstacle and an opportunity. It may be frustrating, but it also lessens the competition. Consumers get so little choice that any firm providing halfway decent goods or services against the odds can do nicely. Smartcard Nigeria, for instance, a joint venture by several Nigerian banks, has developed a welcome alternative to cash. The firm produced an "electronic purse"—a plastic card with a memory chip embedded in it that can be loaded with credit from the customer's bank account. This "virtual money" can then be spent at shops, hotels and restaurants.

The smart card is aimed at Nigeria's middle class, which is small as a proportion of the population, but large in absolute terms. After a successful pilot run in Lagos, involving 24,000 card holders and 200 merchants, the firms managing director, now hopes to attract a million customers within three years. Credit cards, he reckons, will take at least five years to get established in Nigeria. So he predicts handsome profits for his venture.

Another success has been the growth of private airlines. Firms such as Bell view Airlines have take advantage of the low reputation of the national carrier, Nigeria Airways which is to be sold off. Over 99% of passengers on internal flights now use private carriers, which are cheap and fairly reliable. Flying between Nigeria airports is still not as safe as it should be. One hazard is hold-up on runways in which the robbers force open the hold and steal the luggage. Worse, an organization calling itself the "Association of unemployed pilots in Nigeria" recently issued a thinly veiled threat to sabotage airlines that hire foreign pilots instead of locals. Yet Nigeria's airports are less hellish then they were. In the early 1990s, passengers had to hand over fistfuls of bribes to get through customs and passport controls. But on a recent trip, your investigator was asked for nothing more than a ballpoint pen in return for not having his bag searched. And flying is much safer then traveling by road, where potholes, drunken drivers and brigands await travelers. As a Nigerian newspaper put it: "Nigeria roads eat more regularly than battlefields."

GUINNESS MADE GOOD

Some companies have prospered through sheer doggedness. Guinness Nigeria, for example, struggled in the early 1990s as income fell, but it bounced back. By determinedly cutting its costs and squeezing its suppliers, it made a return on 23% on its assets last year. Nigeria is the world's third-biggest market by volume for the company's thick dark beer. The managing director of the firms Nigeria opeation, cites low labour costs, a large market and sexy advertising as reasons for its success. He might also have mentioned the lack of competition. The Nigerian beer market is essentially a duopoly, split between Nigerian Breweries, which is part-owned by Heineken, and Guinness Nigeria. The country's poor infrastructure has put most international brewers off, but Guinness has been selling beer in West African since the 19th century and set up its first brewery in Nigeria in 1962.

In his book "Managing Uncertainty", published in 1998 by spectrum books, Pat Utomi of the Lagos Business School urges that a prerequisite for success in Nigeria has been the ability to adapt to a tickle political environment. Bankers, for instance, have had to cope with the deregulation of interest rates in 1987, re-regulation in 1991 and deregulation again in 1992. Under Abacha, who had no coherent ideas about economics but was able to rule by fiat, policy twirled like a weathervane. One of Abacha's numerous finance ministers announce the lifting of a ban on rice imports, but had a note slipped to him shortly afterwards, when he was making a speech on television, to say that the president had reconsidered and that the ban would remain. Even now, regulations change back and forth, tariffs yo-yo, and permission to do something as innocuous as making a new type of sweet can take six months.

Business can begin to boom in Nigeria only when there is less uncertainty. The present government has shown some commitment to fiscal and monetary discipline, which is a good sign, although without knowing what the oil price will be, the size of the budget deficit is hard to predict. Inflation, it is hoped, will stay within manageable bounds. Bureaucratic delays are being reduced by President Obasanjo's anti corruption crusade. But the most important thing the government can do to get things moving is to privatize the service providers whose incompetence force businesses to resort to 'BYOI'.

Unfortunately the government does not seem to grasp the urgency of this task. Its stakes in firms around the country were to have been sold off by now, but they have been put back to maybe this year or next. Telecoms policy have picked up. The government broke up NITEL'S monopoly and hopes to sell its stake this year. Private firms have been allowed to offer international calls, and even though the license fee for GSM mobile network in Nigeria is a ridiculous $100m, the operating firms in just a short while have all more than not, smiled to the bank. On privatization in general, some economist analyst argue for caution. "it is important to do it right." Says Philip Asiodu, former economic adviser. "We do not want to privatize Russian-Style."

Fair enough. Sales to cronies, or deals that simply transform public monopolies into private ones, will not benefit Nigeria. Bidding must be transparent. Before there can be fair competition in the oil and power markets, clear regulations must be in place. But dawdling incurs its own costs. The sooner publicly owned firms are sold, the sooner the government can start paying off its debts, and perhaps bring interest rate down. The sooner private sector managers are brought into sort out Nigeria's utilities, the sooner Nigeria will be a tolerable place to do business.

COLD COMFORT FARM
BEING POOR IN THE CITY IS GRIM IN THE COUNTRY EVEN GRIMMER

Aeroplanes and smartcards are all very well, but they barely register with Nigeria's large number of poor people. In 1997, one Nigerian in two lived on less than 30 cents a day, says the federal office of statistics. The figures are not all that reliable, but there is little doubt that poverty in Nigeria is widespread and became more so for most of the 1990s. Walk around the slums of Ibadan or Warri, and you will see the destitute densely packed into filthy, dank shacks, dark inside or occasionally lit with a dim kerosene lamp. Many of the urban poor are recent migrants from the countryside. The proportion of Nigerians living in towns swelled from a fifth in 1963 to well over a third in 1991, according to the United Nations development programme. Millions of peasant left their fields in pursuit of a little piece of the country's oil wealth. When successive oil booms bust, many were thrown out of work. Government could no longer afford to pay street cleaners, bureaucrats could no longer afford domestic servants, and the restaurants, nightclubs and shops formerly fuelled by petronaira closed down.

There are still crumbs falling from the tables of the oil-rich, but not as many as before, and more people are pursuing them. Motorists stuck in traffic can buy paw-paws, nuts or a car wash from one of dozens of hawkers. At the golf course in Lagos, where bankers and oil executives relax, a whole hierarchy of crumb catching can be watched in action. It costs about $20 to play; the caddymaster demands $10 for the brief moment it takes him to assign a caddy to each golfer; and the caddies, top of the heap of manual workers, are paid $2 for four hours of humping a heavy bag. Below them in the pecking order come the "sweepers", who for a few coins flatten a path to the hole for the golfer's ball across the bumpy dirt of the putting surface; and then the half naked men who dive into the oil, stagnant water hazard to grope for wayward golf balls, which they clean and sell for a pittance. Add to this the barmen, the boiled egg sellers and the shoe polishers, and the average golfer probably pays ten different people during the course of a single round, and turns away disappointed dozens.

The poor congregate in Nigeria's cities because life in the countryside is grimmer still. It should not be. The country has wonderfully fertile soil, suitable for growing a variety of valuable crops. But after decades of neglect, Nigerian agriculture is falling far short of its potential. For example, large parts of the country offers just the right conditions for growing cocoa beans of exceptionally high quality; and yet cocoa production in Nigeria has tumbled from over 300,000 tones in 1970 to little more than half that last year, in nearby Ghana and Cote d'Iviore, coca is reliable export earner and big employer of rural labour. In Nigeria, it is a sad reminder of the countries wasted opportunities.

Other crops have similarly been allowed to wither. The conditions for growing rubber in Nigeria are ideal, but the country produced perhaps only a tenth as much as it could. Palm oil, used in soap, lubricants and industrial fats, was the staple of Nigeria's commerce with the outside world in the period between the banning of the slave trade and the discovery of petroleum. Today, palm leaves still provide the thatching for Nigerian houses and palm planks the walls, but exports of palm oil are stagnant. In the 1950s. Nigeria supplied Indonesia with its first palm seedlings. In 1970, Indonesia produced half as much palm oil as Nigeria. By 1991, it was producing three times as much and in the mid 1990s Nigeria started to import Indonesian palm oil. Nigeria's export of other formerly lucrative crops, such as groundnuts and cotton have virtually ceased.

MAN MADE MISERY

Nigerian agriculture has been scuppered by a combination of oil and poor policies. The first oil boom brought a sudden flood of foreign currency, much of which went on building swanky new government buildings and making life comfortable for managers at state owned companies. Working in construction and services suddenly became more rewarding than farming, so a lot of peasants threw away their hoes and surged into the cities. At the same time the oil exports strengthened the naira, making other Nigerian exports, such as cash crops less competitive. Even when the boom ended the currency remained overvalued, because the government imposed controls to protect it fearing that devaluation would spark inflation.

Bad policies over the years added to Nigerian farmers' gloom in a number of ways. Subsidies such as those for fertilizer benefited only the middlemen. Marketing boards, to which farmers were obliged to sell most exportable crops, had originally been set up to ensure that farmers got a reasonable price for their produce, but the prices were set too low, so the boards imposed a hefty implicit tax on impoverished peasants. The boards were not abolished until the mid 1980s. that decade also brought a number of import bans, including one on wheat which, along with subsidies for domestic wheat—growing, was meant to stimulate Nigerian Agriculture. Some regions where land was unsuitable for wheat growing grew little or no wheat but pocketed the handouts anyway. A bread shortage followed.

Policy was not only poor, it was also predictable. For farmers who were already subject to the vagaries of the weather and of world commodity prices, that created special difficulties. Not knowing whether the government would manipulate the prices of their products up or down, they were discouraged from investing in higher-yielding crops and more efficient methods of production. The green revolution, which boosted agricultural productivity throughout the developing world, passed Nigeria by.

Under this government, things are looking up a little. The naira is no longer absurdly over-valued, so Nigeria's agricultural exports need not be uncompetitive. But the reintroduction of fertilizer subsidies is a backward step.

Other reforms would be more useful, starting with the simplification of the rules governing land ownership. At present, the state technically owns almost all agricultural land, and farmers have only a vaguely defined right to farm it after several years of incumbency. The system has many local variations, but nowhere is ownership clear enough for small farmers to be able to use the soil as collateral for raising loans to buy better seeds, plant new cocoa trees and generally improve productivity. Other things the government could do include patching up the rural infrastructure, and perhaps encouraging the creation of commodities futures exchange. But what it needs to do more than anything else is to keep its policies consistent.

PICK YOUR PARASITE
NIGERIA IS AN UNHEALTHY PLACE TO LIVE, IN ALL SORTS OF WAYS

Nigeria's climate may be lovely for cocoa trees, but it is harsh for people. In 1805 Mungo Park, a Scottish explorer, led a 45-man expedition to find the source of the river Niger, but illness put an end to the adventure. The only European in the group not to succumb to malaria was Park himself, and some say he was killed by local tribesmen. Nigeria's debilitating heat and swarms of mosquitoes are perhaps the main reason why British colonizers never settle in large numbers. But the conditions are not particularly healthy for local people either. In Nigeria, as in many tropical countries, there is a greater incidence of disease than in more temperate climes. Some economists think this slows down development. Most of the world's poorest countries are in the tropics. Poverty aggravates health problems: the poor often cannot afford vital medicines or adequate food. And poor health, in turn aggravates poverty.

In many parts of Nigeria people are subjected to hundreds of infectious mosquito bites each year, making it hard to avoid contracting malaria. Every workplace is regularly disrupted by it. The health ministry has no idea how many Nigerians die of the disease each year, but reckons that over a million are seriously sickened by it.

Half of the Nigerian population has no access to safe drinking water; many women walk hours everyday to fetch the precious stuff, balancing pots of their heads. Water borne parasites and bacteria thrive. The most deadly consequence is probably diarrhea, which makes 400,000 Nigerians seriously ill each year. The condition is cheat to treat; all it takes is a few cents' worth of rehydration salts. But for poor families living miles from the nearest pharmacy, such remedies are often unavailable.

Nigerian health workers have notched up some successes, for instance against river blindness and guinea worm. About 35m Nigerians live in areas where they risk picking up <u>Onchocerca</u> <u>volvulus</u> parasites that burrow into the eyes and cause blindness. River blindness used to disable huge numbers of Nigerians, but the disease has been brought largely under control by the use of ivermectin, a drug donated by an American drug firm, that kills the pest in its human host. Nigeria's progress in curbing guinea worm, a parasite that can keep its victim off work for months is equally heartening. Microscopic guinea worm egg enters human via water fleas, swallowed when drinking dirty water. The worm grows up to three feet (almost a metre) in length causing fever, pain and fatigue. It can be removed only after it has burst through the skin. The hapless host must then spend weeks or months gently tugging it out. Following a global campaign led by the World Health Organization and others, Nigerians in areas at risk now use filters to strain fleas out of their drinking water. The incidence of guineas worm infestations has dropped from about 700,000 a year a decade ago to about 13,000.

In other respects, however health care in Nigeria has deteriorated. Not until president Obasanjo revamped it systematically, immunization collapsed under the Abacha regime. Basic clinics, long neglected by Nigeria's military rulers in favour of big, prestigious hospitals, are in tatters. It is left to non governmental organizations to teach elementary health precautions to ordinary Nigerians, and to discourage harmful traditions, such as sharing tribal skin-marking knives. The hospitals have crumbled too. Previous governments were generous with the funds to build them, but made little or no allowance for their maintenance or running costs. Budgeting was usually chaotic.

THE WORST IS YET TO COME

The present health sector, has impressed foreign donors with its energy. Unlike in the past, the new team sensibly emphasizes primary care, prevention and inoculation, the measures that save the most lives for the fewest naira. The challenge is immense. Almost a fifth of Nigeria children die before their fifth birthday. Nearly half of the underfives are stunted because of poor nutrition. Mothers have large families an average of six children per women because they expect to lose some of them in infancy. Life expectancy in Nigeria has stuck at about 50 years, and that may soon drop if large numbers of Nigerians start to die to AIDS (God forbid).

The first cases of AIDS in Nigeria were reported in 1986, and surveys conducted in the first half of the 1990s suggested that the virus was spreading rapidly. HIV prevalence among Nigerian adults was estimated to be 1.8% in 1990, 3.8% in 1994 and 4.5% in 1995. Under the past regime, AIDS research was neglected, but a new survey, published in December, found that in the country as a whole 5.4% of adults were infected, and in some areas over 20%. As a percentage of the population, these figures are less dreadful than those in, say, Zimbabwe or Zambia, but because Nigeria has so many people the absolute numbers are staggering: the country can expect at least 5m AIDS deaths in the next ten years, and that may be only the beginning if measures are not taken.

Some Nigerians are aware of the danger. The first death from AIDS of a Nigerian celebrity—the Afro beat star Fela Kuti in 1997—brought grim publicity for the disease. A number of newspaper recently ran frightening (but possible accurate) reports on the level of infection among Nigerian Soldiers returning from peacekeeping duties in Sierra Leone and Liberia. But most Nigerians see AIDS as a disease that afflicts only foreigners, because they have yet to see friends or relatives waste away. "there is no sense of panic yet" says a director of the Association for reproductive and family health in Ibadan. "But there should be."

This government takes the virus seriously, and are working with the world bank to set up a prevention programme. The first step will be to improve the screening of blood for transfusions, which at present account for a significant share of infections. The next step, trying to persuade people to change their sexual habits, will be as tricky in Nigeria as anywhere else. Polygamy is common almost a quarter of married men have two or more wives—and promiscuity and prostitution are widespread. Poverty prevents many Nigerians from taking antibiotics for venereal diseases, and untreated genital sores make HIV transmission more likely. Female genital mutilation, to which about half of Nigerian women have been subjected, can lead to bleeding during sex, which is similarly risky. Only one Nigerian woman in ten practices any form of birth controls, which rarely involves condoms. Many Nigerians remain ignorant of how the virus is transmitted; few realize how widespread it already is.

The impact of AIDS on the Nigerian economy is as yet hard to predict. Output may be affected only gradually. With unemployment high, firms that lose staff will have little trouble replacing them. For the oil industry, which employs a relatively small number of people and imports some of those with essential engineering skills, world oil prices will have a far greater effect on the bottom line. But the effect on the welfare of ordinary Nigerians could be catastrophic. AIDS patients linger before they die, so relatives may have to stop work to look after them. When breadwinners sicken, household incomes plummet just as medical bills soar. In ten years' time, the number of Nigerian children orphaned by AIDS could exceed the total population of neighbouring Benin or Chad. God still forbid! Africa will not become a graveyard in our generation.

FISSIPAROUS FOLKS
"NIGERIA HAS NOT ONLY A NORTH-SOUTH DIVIDE, BUT A MULTITUDE OF OTHER FAULT LINES TOO"

In October 1999, Ahmed Sani, the governor of Zamfara, declared that his small northern State would henceforth be subject to Sharia (Islamic) law, citing Saudi Arabia as his model. He has encouraged the growing of beards, although they are not being made mandatory, and banned prostitution and the sale of alcohol. Thieves will have their hands cut off, but only in "extreme" cases. The announcement caused uproar. Despite Governor Sani's assurances that Sharia courts would try only members of Zamfara's Muslim majority, the state's Christian minority was terrified. Muslim leaders who favour a secular state were afraid to speak out for fear of being branded un-Islamic, a label that could prove hazardous. Newspapers, most of which are Christian-owned, condemned the move, predicting that it would spark an exodus of Christian and lead to the break-up of the country. So far this has happened, but in February 2000 Kaduna state said it, too, would adopt Sharia. Crisis broke out repeatedly causing the deaths of thousands of innocent souls and destruction of properties that can't be quantified. Churches were burnt down, mosques were destroyed and reprisal started in other states. Kano state said it, too, would adopt Sharia. Other majority Muslim states followed. The debate highlights one of Nigeria's most enduring problems holding together a country with such a diverse and fractions populations.

Northern Nigeria is mainly Muslim. The south is mainly Christian and animist. The middle belt is mixed. Nigerians sometimes refer to the "mistake of 1914", when British colonial cartographers united northern and southern Nigeria by the stroke of a pen. Antagonism between north and south is not simply about religion: it is a tribal matter, too, with deep historical roots. The British sought to avoid religious turmoil by discouraging Christian missionaries from trying to convert northerners. As an unintended consequence, almost all of Nigeria's western-style schools were built in the south, and business in both the north and the south was also dominated by southerners. By contrast, the army was mainly the preserve of northerners, because the British thought they made better leaders.

The northern officers first seized power in 1966, ostensible to prevent tribal and religious differences from tearing the country apart. Privately they also feared that, with the British gone, wealthier, better-educated southerners would quickly come to dominate the whole country. The northern generals, insecurity also colored their economic policies. According to the world Bank, "Northern elites feared that they would lose in an unrestricted commercial contest, so they used the state to restrict the operation of market capitalism."

SUBDIVIDE AND RULE

The north-south divide is not the only fault line in Nigeria. The country is home to at least 250 ethnic groups, many of whom seem to dislike each other and are keen to let everybody know about it.

Nigerian comedians play endlessly on ethnic stereotypes: Yorubas are noisy. Ibos are tight-fisted and Hausas are dim, to list only the three most common.

Between 1967 and 1970 the south eastern part of Nigeria tried to secede. The discovery of oil in the region may have added to the fervour with which the Ibos, the largest ethnic group there, fought for an independent "Biafra" and the equal fervour with which the northern Moslem fought to keep Nigeria intact. But the Biafran war was mainly about ethnic and religious difference. Rightly a million people died, mainly of war-induced starvation and disease. Desperate to prevent a repeat, subsequent governments have worked hard to appease ethnic interest, sometimes with bizarre results.

Small ethnic groups, hoping to lay their hands on more of the oil money, have split the Nigerian federation into ever smaller chunks, from four regions in 1963 to 36 states today. This has caused endless complexity. For instance, state government hoping to privatize state owned firms often find that the state which originally set up the firm has been split into several small ones, none of whose leaders can agree on how to proceed. Politicians habit of giving jobs and contracts to their own ethnic groups fosters what Chinua Achebe calls a "cult of mediocrity." In Nigeria, he says, "it would be difficult to point to one important job held by the most competent person we have."

Communalism has prevented the emergence of political parties based on ideology. When allowed to vote, Nigerians have tended to support someone from their own ethnic group, which means that politicians do not need ideas to get elected. Tribal loyalty also explains why so many Nigerians have shamelessly plundered the state. According to Eghosa Osaghae, a political historian, many Nigerians regarded the state itself as an alien transplant.

IT IS A POPULAR NIGERIAN SAYING, WHICH TOOK ROOT UNDER COLONIAL RULE, THAT "GOVERNMENT'S BUSINESS IS NO MAN'S BUSINESS.

THERE WAS THUS NOTHING SERIOUSLY WRONG WITH STEALING STATE FUNDS, ESPECIALLY IF THEY WERE USED TO BENEFIT NOT ONLY THE INDIVIDUAL BUT ALSO MEMBERS OF HIS COMMUNITY.

President Obasanjo, a Biafran veteran himself, sincerely wants to ease tensions. A Yoruba who drew most of his electoral support from non—yorubas, he is one of the few Nigerian politicians whose loyalties are not determined by his tribal origins. He is now trying to divide federal funds more equitably among the state while reducing incentives for further division. His swollen cabinet contains at least one member from each of the 36 states. But it is impossible to satisfy everyone.

Since Federal money is, at least in theory, allocated to states on the basis population, Nigerian census have in the past been marred by fraud and violence as each group sought to inflate its numbers. Nobody really knows how many people Nigeria has. The last census, in 1991, put the total at 88.5m. In 1998, the government's estimate was 108.5m and the United Nations' 121.8m. Most tribes say they have been undercounted and underpaid, maybe the 2005 census will give the correct figures.

Since the end of military rule, communal violence has increased, perhaps because the police no longer suppress it so forcefully. Christians fight Muslims in the north, Ijaws and Itsekiris torch each others homes in the Niger Delta, Yoruba youths (aka OPC) lob "magic bombs"—egg shells filled with sulphuric acid at members of other tribes in Lagos. Since President Obasanjo came into office, at least 20,000 people have died in ethnic clashes. Some observers predict that Nigeria will fall apart like Yugoslavia or Congo; but most Nigerians trust that the country will somehow muddle through. Bishop David Oyedepo, head of one of the country's largest Charismatic Christian churches and a friend of President Obasanjo, reckons that "if the country was going to break up, it would already have done so. Things were worse under Abacha. People are more optimistic now."

A story from Kaduna gives grounds for optimism. In the early 1990s two religious terrorist. Mohammed Ashafa and James Wuye, tried to have each other killed during a burst of communal blood letting, for which Mr. Ashafa blamed the Christian paramilitary group led by Mr. Wuye, and Mr. Wuye blamed Mr. Ashafa's uncle, thinking it was Mr. Ashafa. Muslim assassins attacked Mr. Wuye, hacked his arm off and left him for dead. Both men believed they had eliminated the other. When they later discovered they had not, they set up a joint charity to promote dialogue between Christians and Muslims. They are now the best of friends.

UMPTEENTH TIME LUCKY
ANOTHER CHANCE TO MAKE NIGERIA WORK

Nigerians dream of a national revival; of a new Nigeria where shoddiness is no longer the norm; where electrical firms boast of something more ambitious than that their wiring will not burn your house down. They want to live in a place where hotels no longer feel obliged to warn each new guest to beware of kidnappers passing as chauffeurs; where mineral wealth is no longer divided among the few while tens of millions live in squaler; and where, instead of being trampled by soldiers, citizens breath what president Obasanjo once called "the air of absolute freedom." This dream is not exactly new. It had previous outings after the changes of government in 1960, 1966, (twice), 1975, 1979, 1983, 1985 and, in a small way in 1993. Each time the dreamers had a rude awakening. Why should now be any different?

There are good reasons for predicting that the latest government, like its predecessors, will fail to live up to any of these hopes. For Nigeria to becomes a stable democracy, it must become less poor. Growth from upswings in the oil price is not enough, because what goes up can come down, it must come from steady investment in higher productivity, which can last and sustain itself. But it takes time and diligence to set up and operate a textile factory or a rubber plantation, and Nigerians are not patient. Just as 70 years of communism warped Russian culture in ways that cannot be straightened out overnight, so decades of keptocracy have entrenched the get-rich-quick mentality in Nigeria. So many fortunes were made so fast and with such ease, that many Nigerians now consider this normal. An eye for an instant profit is a useful quality in a trader, which is perhaps why Nigeria's markets are so lively. However, it takes different talents to farm, to make something people want to buy, or to run a government that enables citizens to thrive, rather than stealing their money and strangling their businesses with controls.

A life time of being ripped off has understandably, made Nigerian's hungry for compensation. Watching oligarchs grow fat by grabbling a piece of the oil money has convinced many of them that their country's problems could be solved by sharing out the oil revenue more equitably.

It would be a start, of course. But even if Nigeria's oil bounty were shared out with mathematical precision, Nigerians would still be poor. Assume an oil price of $25 a barrel, no operating costs, and no money spent on distributing. Two million barrels a day would yield $50m to be shared between 100m people, so everyone would get 50 cents. A lot of Nigerians would be delighted to receive an extra 50 cents a day, but it would not bring them water, light, education or health care; that would still require lots of Nigerians to learn how to lay pipes, maintain pylons, deliver text books and manage health budgets efficiently. Nigeria cannot depend on oil forever. To prosper in the long term, it must learn now to create wealth, rather than simply extracting it from the soil.

Ethnic jealousies have doubtless continue to reinforce the Nigerian tendency to bicker over the division of the oil spoils rather than devise other ways of making money. Those who benefited from corruption in the past will try to frustrate the present governments reform effort. Ambitious colonels may be waiting for an opportunity to grab power back again. Members of the new national assembly seem more concerned with the size of their furniture allowances than with the size of the national debt. In these circumstances, what chance is there of a prosperous Nigeria?

I SEE HOPE!

"I see hope" was the title of President Obasanjo's book. Optimism you would say. However in the economist prints of this survey. This paragraph reads "Maybe, just maybe."

Do not dismiss the idea out of hand. Granted, many aspects of Nigerian culture are inimical to growth. But cultures change, particularly when incentives do. Compare China under Mao with China under Deng Xiaping. President Obasanjo may not yet have embraced radical reform, but he is clearly trying to change things for the better. Encouraging, formerly critical outsiders agree. When Transparency International smiles on a Nigerian President, that is reason for optimism. Economists grouch that the president is not liberalizing or privatizing quickly enough, and they are right. But at least he has promised to do all of these things. Remember, too, that most Nigerians found the status quo unacceptable; and that the rest of the world would dearly love to see an African success story involving a country more populous than Botswana.

Nigeria is potentially rich, Nigerians never tire of telling visitors. To cynics, that sounds a euphemism for "not rich at present', or "poor and run by crooks." But Nigerians" self-confidence can be exhilarating to behold. Many of them seem to believe that their country is a super power which just happens to have lost its way; that with better leadership Nigeria will quickly become a beacon for Africa. Maybe, just maybe, this exuberance can translate into a Nigeria that works. The country has a better chance now than perhaps at any time since independence. It must not waste it again. Let's keep working at it.

2

'BUSINESS OR PLEASURES'

BUSINESS OR PLEASURES

WEALTH FLOWS TOWARDS A PARTICULAR DIRECTION—IN THE DIRECTON OF THE ENTREPRENEUR—

As I earlier said, it could be very frustrating to know what you want, but don't know how to get it when I searched out the story behind the story of those I term financial giants, I only deduced that wealth flowed in a particular direction—the direction of the entrepreneur and (or) business owner or still the investor. May it be that they have enough courage and boldness to become what they really wanted to be? Well I call them the "wealth creation experts" and sometime the business mastermind. This folks are among the biggest financial giants of all time. They were and are all business people. At the later part of this book I included a few whose stories have some really far touching effects on our lives today and we could learn from them still.

"WE SHOULD KEEP IN MIND THAT THE HUMANITIES COME BEFORE THE DOLLARS. OUR FIRST DUTY RUNS TO MAN BEFORE BUSINESS, BUT WE MUST NOT FORGET THAT SOME-TIMES THE TWO ARE INTERCHANGEABLE"

—Bernard Baruch

I want to hope that this second chapter will arouse that entrepreneurial spirit in you. So let me begin by asking the following questions:

What is an enterprise? And who is an entrepreneur?

An enterprise is a business venture, usually implying one or an element of risk. An entrepreneur is one who organizes and operates a business, usually implying one who is willing to accept risk in the quest for profit.

The word entrepreneur originally means "someone who undertakes a challenge". But of course now it has come to mean anyone who undertakes a business venture, who sees a need and tries to fill it.

Now, from the above definitions, we would see that the key word is 'Risk'. Risk is somewhat like the determining factor; it is the dividing line between courage and mediocrity.

To some decree, I would say that life is all about risk. Anyone who is scared of taking risk, as it has been found is riskier than taking risk, itself. Don't get me wrong; I'm talking about calculated risk not foolish risk.

"THE GAMBLING KNOWN AS BUSINESS LOOKS WITH AUS- TERE DISFAVOUR UPON THE BUSINESS KNOWN AS GAM- BLING"

—Ambrose Gwinneth Bierce.

John Roger and Peter McWilliams in their book: Do it! Have this to say about TAKING RISK!

—As often as we are counseled to "take risk" by the successful people of the world; that's about as often as that counsel is ignored. For the vast, vast major- ity of people, taking risk is just too, well risky.

If you don't take risk, however, its doubtful we'll ever get to our Dream. "A lot of successful people are risk—takers", Philip Adams wrote, "unless you're willing to do that, to have a go to fail miserable and have another go success won't happen".

There must be something risky between you and your dream, otherwise, why wouldn't you be living it? Attaining dreams requires new behavior and new behavior is taking risk.

"Be daring, be different, be impractical, "Sir Cecil Beaton advised, "Be any- thing that will assert integrity of purpose and imaginative vision against the play—it—safer, the creatures of the common place, the slave of the ordinary".

"There are risks and costs for a programme of action", John E. Kennedy said, "but they are far less than the long range risks and costs of comfortable inactions.

Of course there are limits Andy Warhol had a suggestion for Kennedy and his kind: "The president has so much good publicity potential that hasn't been exploited. He should just sit down one day and make a list of all the things that people are embarrassed to do that shouldn't be embarrassed to do and then do them all on television".

A great idea from Mr. Warhol. Unfortunately, none of our presidents have taken him up on it—not intentionally at any rate.

The irony is that the person not taking risks feels the same amount of fear as the person who regularly takes risks the non—risk taker simply feels the same amount of fear over more trivial things.

Understand that failure is part of the process. We told you about our publishing success but have told you about our failures? To quote Jack Benny, "Well!" they were something.

People not taking calculated risks, designed to pursue their dream, sometimes take foolish risks. They drive too fast, drink too much, abuse drugs or engage in some other reckless behavior. "Take calculated risk", George Patton advised, "That is quite different from being rash".

Maybe the risk taking mechanism in these rash individuals need to be exercised or maybe they want to prove (to themselves as much to others) that they're not so cowardly after all. If they really wanted to display their courage, all they'd have to do is pursue their dreams.

The reverse of that is more often true. Having given up on their dreams, many give up on life and die a little more each day.

As Benjamin Franklin wrote, "Some people die at twenty five and aren't buried until they are seventy five". Or to quote Auntie Mame's famous line, "life is a banquet, and some poor sons—of—bitches are starving to death".

The thing we fear: all you have to do is walk right up and confront it. It's among the hardest things to do, but it the only thing to be done. If you turn from it, it will bite you in the butt. The further you run from it, the further you run from your dream. "Do the things you fear", wrote Emerson, and the death of fear is certain".

"Often the difference between a successful man and a failure is not one's better abilities or ideas", Maxwell Maltz observed, "but the courage that one has to bet on his ideas to take a calculated risk—and to act".

"WHERE THERE'S NO RISK THERE'S NO PRIDE IN ANY THING YOU DO, SO THERE CAN BE NO HAPPINESS IN IT".

—Ray Kroc

I once saw an article on risk that I love so much.
"it's a simple truth—anything you do involve risk.
To drive a car is to risk having a wreck.
To apply for a job is to risk not being hired.
To try out for a play is to risk not getting the part.
To enter college is to risk flunking out.
To smile is to risk that no one will smile back.
To love is to risk rejection and hurt.
To speak is to risk that no one will listen.
To hope is to risk despair.
To dream is to risk appearing the fool
To climb is to risk falling back down.

One ingredient I've noticed in the personality of almost every successful person I know is the courage to risk failure. To try is definitely to risk failure, but what is your alternative? To do nothing have nothing and be nothing. When you do absolutely nothing you've avoided failure, but you also have avoided success. Anything of important in life involves risk; if you don't try you can't do. Don't be afraid to reach for your dreams. As will Rogers once said, "You've got to go on a limb sometimes because that's where the fruit is!

"THE MISFORTUNE HARDEST TO BEAR ARE USUALLY THOSE WHICH NEVER HAPPENED"

—James Russell Lowell.

Well, I am advocating that every one become a businessperson over night? Just to free our society of all her present dilemma? Yes! I'm saying exactly that. More importantly, I'm saying that if you want to be free to attract real solid wealth, become a businessperson. Let me at this junction come to another simple but sensitive question:

What is business? And who is a businessman?

Business is an enterprise established to provide a product or service in the hope of earning a profit. Such an enterprise may be a sole proprietorship, a partnership or a corporation.

A businessman therefore, is a man that is busy with a worthwhile pursuit.

"THE GOALS OF BUSINESS ARE INSEPERABLE FROM THE GOALS OF THE WHOLE COMMUNITY. EVERY ATTEMPT TO SEVER THE ORGANIC UNITY OF BUSINESS AND THE COMMUNITY INFLICTS EQUAL HARDSHIP ON BOTH".

—Earl Bunting

ENTREPRENEURSHIP DEVELOPMENT

Developing the entrepreneurial spirit among Africans especially the young people is going to restore back, African economic dignity. That's what I'm preaching I'm saying more and more Africans need to build their own companies and become employers of labour even has they establish their dreams. People will vision and courage need to step out and build companies that will in the near future become a fortune—500 company.

Have you ever sensed the entrepreneurial spirit come into you? Do you see yourself has a capitalist or at least a potential capitalists? Or are you angry about capitalism. You may think that capitalists are too greedy with gain, they are cruel and exploitative. But it's not all of them. Some of them are the most generous, loving and caring people in the world. I think you should be one, a 'capitalist' or if the label scares you too much, call yourself an entrepreneur or a free enterpriser or even still a compassionate capitalist.

One way or the other, I plead with you to participate in this great free enterprise system. We will benefit enormously from it's advantages or else we will miss our chances forever. We must know and believe that the spirit of free enterprise flows through our body and can work for Africans as it did work for America. Have you heard of the Rockefellers, Carnegies, Hiltons, Fords, Gates, Turners, Devos etc This entrepreneurial spirit was born right inside of us, just like our need to eat and drink, to love and be loved, to learn, to grow and to achieve.

Truth is entrepreneurs are not in a secret cult. Anyone can be an entrepreneur. Age is no barrier. Young people who organize a school play, write essays on paper, sing on stage, sell fruits, pick up one or two casual jobs down the streets are all entrepreneurs. Student of universities, polytechnics, colleges of educations and higher learning institutions can be entrepreneurs. Adults of any age including senior and the very senior citizens can be entrepreneurs. Gender is not an issue. Men and women are all equally gifted with the same entrepreneurial spirit. When it comes to entrepreneurship there are no limiting barriers whatsoever except those we impose on ourselves.

When did you first notice your entrepreneurial spirit? Did the spirit of free enterprise move you to start a soft drink stand on the road side, sell oranges and sugarcane after school period, sell groundnuts and vegetables from the front of your house? Or like most recently start a GSM call point? May be you use digger and shovel to work on a construction or farm site. Do you sell newspapers or you wash cars. Just to mention but a few. Whatever thing, you've been telling yourself that there is more to life than just eating and drinking. You have also been telling yourself that it is like war out there on the street, but there is more out there.

But you know that your potential is infinite and you need to be wise and be able to visualize. You are condensing to this simple and clear truth: "own your own business boy it's the only way to be free". Yes I know it will be hardwork, but you'll be making more money than you hard ever dreamed. All successful entrepreneurs have a positive attitude about work. They will say 'work is just work', but they will always tell you that for them, most work is interesting.

May be you don't want to own a business, but you feel the entrepreneurial spirit moving inside of you. That's okay. Too many people thinking that entrepreneurs have to own their own business and that by working for someone else they kill their entrepreneurial spirit. That's not correct. As a matter of fact, there are very many creative gifted people who like working in other people's businesses large or small. They don't feel too comfortable with the responsibility that comes with going out on their own. They like the regular monthly pay than the risk that goes with starting one's own business. They'd rather be in a large community of workers than alone.

Just for the sake of clarity, perhaps we should call employees who do more than just the messengers job "professionals". More and more business and even profession are beginning to find new creative ways to honor the contributions made by these employees who let their entrepreneurial spirit lead the way. Such professionals ask certain questions and act on them accordingly:—

1. What can I do in my current job, business or profession to grew to use my gifts and talent more creativity to feel more satisfied with what I do each day?

2. How can I help make the business stronger more successful?

3. What would make this task more efficient less time consuming and thus less expensive?

4. How can we improve the work place to make it safer, more relaxed more comfortable for me and for my fellow workers?

5. What are we doing wrong? How could we do it better?

We can spend our lives just putting in our time on the job, but the entrepreneurs and professionals see work everyday as an opportunity to grow, create discover, challenge old ideas and come up with new and better ones.

We always like the interesting stories of entrepreneurs who own their own business but do not forget, there are employees who work in the offices and plants of these businesses around the world. Without the commitments and creativity of those employees or should I say professionals now, no business can survive. Business owners have to understand the creativity and commitment of these employees as they too have the skill and gift to own their own business, but they choose to share their talents with you and so be grateful to them. They have a unique perspective and so through proper human relation skills you can learn a lot from them especially concerning the inside of the business and outside environment.

When you reach out to employees, they reach back to you. Without their loyalty, their creative ideas and their hard work no business and enterprise will succeed. Be careful: the larger we grow the easier it becomes to take people for granted and the harder it becomes to stay in touch.

MOULDING AFRICAN ENTREPRENEURS

I spell E-N-T-R-E-P-R-E-N-E-U-R as R-I-S-K. Some say there is so much fun in extreme sport. But we are not just talking about extreme sport here; we are talking about calculated risk. The risk whereby you know what you hope to achieve in the pursuit of it. And until you get that which you hope to achieve, life becomes more and more meaningless.

The true entrepreneur is a risk taker. And to be excellent in taking risk you need one major quality that will make all the difference for you. That quality is called CONFIDENCE. You need self-confidence.

"BY ALLOWING FULL SCOPE FOR INVESTMENT, MOBILTY, THE DIVISION OF LABOUR, CREATIVITY AND ENTREPRE-NEURSHIP, THE FREE ECONOMY THEREBY CREATES THE CONDITIONS FOR RAPID ECONOMIC DEVELOPMENT"

—Murray Rothbard.

It is not an easy process to just transmute a desire to money—you must first be sure and convinced that you really need to do everything physically to achieve your desired goal. Once this is been engraved at the back of your mind the itching desires will be backed with planning and progressive plan of actions for the actualization of your purposeful goal.

A person without a plan and who is without self-confidence will lead a life of purposelessness and randomly misdirected energy, which will altogether add up to zero.

The true entrepreneur needs to have faith in both himself as well has in what he is producing. And we know that faith is what brings the spiritual importance of our desired goal. As an entrepreneur works out his/her plans step by step, they see their destination get closer and so their confidence is built stronger.

"ASSUREDNESS IS THE ONLY KNOWN ANTIDOTE FOR FAILURE"

—Hill.

The entrepreneur respects the system. He loves man and knows that man is the only real sources of riches. And that the only way to make money is by providing something that benefits all the people involved in any non-forceful voluntary transaction. He benefits, others benefit.

The linking dots behind every fortune are more than just simple motivations. Riches come when desire is coupled with a goal, plan and lots of hard work.

Financial success is achieved through a four-part formula. First you must plan, then save, finally invest and always compound. No one can succeed without a plan. And then be motivated to execute that plan. He becomes successful when he reaches his goals, or passes by each sub goal within the budgeted time frame. One of the best ways to painlessly save is by taking at least 10% out of every thing that comes into your hands before you even start spending your money.

John D. Rockefeller only earned $13.46 a week as a wholesale clerk. He didn't smoke, drink or play pool. And he saved $1,000 in just two and a half years enough money for the then 19 years old to go into a business partnership.

From our earliest childhood days until we grow too old to dream, we are hounded by important questions. Edison, Bell, Ford and the great entrepreneur and business master minds in the past asked and answered themselves these same questions. Bill gates, Jerry Yang, Ted Turner and other present billionaires who dared to form business of their own while most other people went on dreaming. Looking at a simple list, are the questions below, ones you've been asking yourself? Where do these questions come from? God? Conscience? The entrepreneurial spirit? Finding the sources of these questions isn't nearly as important as finding the courage to answer them.

THE QUESTIONS

1.   How can I create money and feel more financially secure?

2.   What kind of work will make me feel best about myself?

3.   What have I always dreamed of doing and why don't I do it?

4.   Would starting my own business help me get solutions to this question?

5.   If so what kind of business would I like to start, to own, to build?

Answering these questions with honesty and courage has led million of people to take one of the most exiting worthwhile steps a woman or man can take. They looked closely at their dissatisfactions and dreams. They wanted to be free, to be their own boss, to control their lives again. They wanted financial security for themselves and for the people they loved. They wanted to use their creativity to develop their gifts and end the cycle of poverty and boredom that had them feeling trapped and tired all the time. For my friends in Nigeria and for tens of millions like them across Africa, the answer is to start a business of their own.

Since success isn't measured with money alone, you need a business that will allow you have time to spend with those you love. And because you are free to set your own priorities and what to spend you money for you are also free to use your money and gifts in showing love to others across the countries by building foundations and charities that will support such course.

We will read endless stories inside of men and women who did just that to make America a great nation today.

In good and bad economic times, millions of people dream of owing a business one day and many of such see their dreams come true. If the spirit of free enterprise has been raising questions in your mind if you've been longing for financial security if you don't like what you're presently doing this is a great time to make a change. I'm not just selling an empty can here. Look around the globe all the developed nations are those that have fully embraced free enterprise and the developing ones are those that are now presently embracing it too. We cannot leave the destiny of this great continent to chance. If we do we will miss our chance. Life is not a chance game but it is choice. Opportunities for entrepreneurs to see their dreams come true are abundant even in these difficult economic times.

AS I SEE CHANGES.

Let me begin by saying we have far too many Africans that have stock piled enough money abroad in western banks and western economies. You would not completely blame them, the lack of security and lack of confidence that we have in our homes countries are part of the major causes for this. Howbeit, if we say we really want a change, we must begin to look inward as individuals or groups. The irony of the whole issue is that most of the money these individuals stock piled were generated and salted away from the wealth of their homeland. Whichever way, these figures are far above what averagely we can imagine, running into millions of dollars in cash and assets abroad. If the poor countries of Africa say they want debt relief from these western countries, the implication is that they (the western world) know of individuals and groups of individuals who are from these so called poor countries but have successfully stock piled too much money in those same western countries and so they become so reluctant as they wonder how. We need to look inward for some really quality changes.

From my rough statistics and calculations, if we can have say fifty or more people invest at least one to fifty million dollars and above directly into the economy of our country, just within one year over 500,000 new businesses, both small and medium and large ones would have been incorporated nationwide. This will account for ninety percent of the net job growth. Of course the number of women who owned businesses would definitely increase simultaneously by say fifty percent with the same period.

The number of business that will be owned by the no graduate degree people would also increase by say 30% in the same given period. The receipt from abroad of all these business would also increase by more than a hundred percent. Where does all this keep us: better standard of living, greater job opportunity reduction in poverty especially among women and the unschooled, higher GDP and GNP. A richer nation, crime reduction a better economy and trust in the future of this country. Less I forget to say that these facts and figures were keep at their least possible out come. So we could work magic. But I'm not just talking magic here; I'm talking about common sense and common decency.

Some folks start a business because they've lost their job after a lifetime of service. They want to feel secured the second or third time around and they discovered that owing their own business though risky and difficult at first meets that need. Others are leaving their jobs and starting their own business because they are bored, disappointed, angry, exhausted or just still tired of corporate life. Some young people fresh out of universities and institution of higher learning are starting their own business. At least most students will tell you that "owning a business gives an excellent opportunity for a successful career". They want freedom and autonomy. They want to direct their energies in any direction they want, to do things the way they want it. They want to identify a need in their community and create business to fill it. Ultimately they want to be free and do what they want to do with their lives.

Caution! Don't get me wrong. There are plenty of business failures everyday. At least Twenty percent of the 500,000 new businesses I envisaged are likely bound in that direction and ten percent of all existing ones may also go under.

Although we don't pray for misfortune, still Rich Devos encourages most people who are thinking of starting a business to consider the following actions:

1. If you have a job, keep it while you start your own business.(you'll be surprised how much extra time and energy you have left in the evenings and on weekends to get a new business going without ever taking time from your current job).

2. Quit your old job when you have enough money stockpiled to keep you through the low—income days ahead.

3. Try to find or create a business opportunity that takes the smallest possible amount of start—up capital.(don't go deep into dept on a whim. Businesses don't need fancy office space, expensive equipment, and dozens of workers in the beginning. Think small, think inexpensive).

4. Be sure that the goods or service you want to manufacture or market are first—class quality.(don't cheat your customers. It leads to certain business failures).

5. Be sure that you know what you are doing, that you have read every possible resource about your new business, that you have talked to a banker, a lawyer, and a friend or two you trust for their common sense. You will learn plenty by trial and error, but know all you can before you start.

Really, don't be scared to try. Remember, in spite of the economic downturns, small and medium scale businesses income increased with some good percentages this year and all across this country and even around the world new businesses are booming. It isn't going to be easy especially if it's your first try. But always remember this: "opportunities are missed by so many people because they are dressed—up in overalls that look like hard work". But even hard work can't kill a man if it comes with a sense of achievement and security that can raise the quality of your life in ways you only dreamed of.

Another piece of advice; before you consider joining any job or business, check it out! Be sure that the business and its people have integrity. Beware of fraudsters who come to you with all sort of juicy opportunities. It's not all that glitters that is gold,—verify every move and contact person's' with the police, your lawyer, corporate associations and all relevant agencies. I think no business can really exist in a vacuum, so check the associations she belongs to and the agencies responsible, and verify the names and reputation of those you want to deal with.

Don't you ever put money where the coast and air surrounding it as not been properly cleared by relevant agencies and authorities. It will save you a whole lot of trouble. Make the idea and the person's' pass the test and that you could trust the individual or company and it's allies to deliver on their promises. Also if you are the one starting your business always tries to follow the legal procedure required for such a business. If you are supposed to Register with legally instituted agencies like NAFDAC, custom duties and the rest of them, please and please, make sure you do just that. Consult them properly, join associations in those sectors and don't try to exist in a vacuum. Do business legally because there are a million and one ways to make money legally, you don't have to make it illegally.

WHAT SUCCESSFUL ENTREPRENEURS DO!

Why are successful entrepreneurs so well rewarded financially in our world today? It's because they add more value than virtually anyone around them. There are two primary benefits that entrepreneurs create.

First, they obviously add value to their customers by increasing the quality of their lives through the use of their product. This, by the way, is critical for any company to prosper. So often, companies forget that their real purpose, for being is not just to make a profit while a profit is an absolute must for a company to survive and flourish—like eating or sleeping, a necessity—it's not the real purpose. The true purpose of any corporation is to create products and services that increase the quality of life for all the customers they serve. If this is achieved on a consistent basis, then profit is absolutely assured. However, a company can profit in the short term and not be around anymore in the long term if it doesn't continually add value to people's lives. This holds true for corporations as much as individuals.

The second thing that entrepreneurs do is that, in creating their products, they create jobs. Because of these jobs, the employee's children can go to school and on to higher education then become doctors, lawyers, teachers, social workers, and add more value to the society s a whole—not to mention the fact that these families spend the money that they earn with other vendors. So the chain of value is never-ending. When an American by name Ross Perot was asked for the secret of his wealth, he said, "what I can do for this country is create jobs. I'm pretty good at that, and lord knows we need them." The more value you contribute, the more you will earn if you put yourself in the position to do so.

One of the most powerful ways of adding value is understanding that in today's society, wealth is created by distribution, products and services are changing constantly, but those who've figured a way to take something of tremendous value and deliver it to a mass number of people will prosper. This has been the secret of the richest man in the United States. He became wealthy by creating a distribution system. Ross Perot did the same thing with information at EDS. If you can figure out how to take something that already has great value and distribute it to people, or distribute it at a lower cost, then you've found another way of adding value. Adding value is not just creating products; "it's finding a way to make sure that more people experience an increase in the quality of life".

Why most people don't do well financially is basically for two reasons:

1. They have limiting beliefs
2. They want something for nothing.

Avoid both if you must make it in this fast paced and ever-changing world.

"WEALTH IS THE PRODUCT OF MAN'S CAPACITY TO THINK"

—Ayn Rand.

IN NIGERIA

Chinua Achebe, internationally acclaimed author, wrote in his book "The trouble with Nigeria" about problems of contemporary Nigeria. Though the book published quite about two decade's back talks hard about Nigeria being destroyed by bad leadership, corruption and inequality. The information's there are still relevant and by reading it, you could literally become sick of this country. But still, he had a message of hope. It's unfortunate that we find ourselves in this awkward system, but never let your mind be affected by what Ziglar calls "stinking thinking" because that really fast turns into a case of "hardening of the attitudes". That's really bad because when you travel all over this country and get to know Nigeria and Nigerians, you will become totally excited about her and completely dedicated to Nigeria.

Obviously, ninety percent of us can't take good trips walking around the country, but by listening to positive comments, reading good books and magazines, and taking an optimistic views of good things that are happening in Nigeria, I believe you, too, will be just as sold on Nigeria as I am. When this happens you will recognize the beauty and the tremendous possibilities Nigeria offers you. As a result, you zest and enthusiasm for life will be rekindled, which means you will work your way to the top. So read at least one positive article (magazine or newspaper) about our great land and share at least one positive comment about our country each day starting from today. Those who don't care to love our native country need only to reside for some time in a foreign one and the difference would be clear.

"THE FUTURE IS NOW"

This could just be the wake-up call to all well-meaning individuals in this country, to awaken the giant within them. Let's stop waiting for the government to do everything for us, lets start doing things for the government. Because that's the only way things will work much better. It will interest you to know that the economy of any society and the standard of living of the citizens are always better off in a business minded environment. This is because everyone will be trying hard to make things work better for himself, and by so doing, they are inevitable making things work better for the community as a whole.

"I DO NOT BELIEVE GOVERNMENT CAN RUN ANY BUSINESS AS EFFICIENTLY AS PRIVATE ENTERPRISE, AND THE VICTIM OF EVERY SUCH EXPERIMENT IS THE PUBLIC"
—Thomas E. Dewey.

That is why, I believe that deregulation and privatization are not the problem now; these are the best things that can happen to our society now. What actually should be a problem is maybe the style which the government is using to approach it is highly questionable. If government can ensure that it's refineries are fairly working, sell them to private bodies and give licenses to the building of even more refineries to private individuals it would be a better approach still. This will be good so that these private individuals will not capitalize on one loop hole or the other and inflict hardship on Nigerians. Products will be refined here in town and the market flooded with it, it's all good. But whichever way the government must eventually take her hands off the business of business for any meaningful development to occur.

In another option still, government can decide to create a strategic oil reserve. In such an instance, anytime greedy businessmen want to create artificial scarcity in the market, which will of course jump shoot the fuel price, he (government) can now decide to flood the market with it's strategic reserves so as to keep prices at a reasonable low level.

Of course prices will be determined by the market, but whatever the government can do to help the public afford these products at a reasonable price it should do. Government should make sure she establishes quality law and agencies to check monopoly and questionable business practices if privatization will make any sense to us. For sure this country cannot continue to rely on importations of virtually everything including oil which she produces-what an irony. Folks lets put our brains on the ground and think, by allowing free enterprise and free market system, individuals can set up strong businesses that will create jobs and generate wealth for the community. Free enterprise has the answers to our future, for our nation, for our children and for even generations unborn. It's the best thing that can happen to this country now.

I think we need to consider Dewey's critical observation especially in most African countries where it seems that every business managed by the governments does not function efficiently. I'm not saying here that the government should shy away from its responsibility to the people, what I'm saying is for governments to redefine it's responsibility so as to create avenue and opportunities for creative individuals to discover their real abilities and live a fulfilling life on our continent.

I will also strongly advise that banks and venture capitalist be organized in such a way so as to aid and give start up capital to these young creative individuals who have dared to live their dreams. The pocket of the citizens determines the economy of a state and it's not the state's economy that determines the pocket of the citizens. If you dare to be rich, if you hate poverty with a passion, if you really want to succeed in life and enjoy financial independence, then you must go the way of the entrepreneur, investor and business owner.

"THE MAN WHO MAKES AN APPEARANCE IN THE BUSINESS WORLD, THE MAN WHO CREATES PERSONAL INTEREST, IS THE MAN WHO GETS AHEAD. BE LIKED AND YOU WILL NEVER WANT"

—Arthur Miller.

UNDERSTANDING PRIVATIZATION; AN EASY ILLUSTRATION

A young man bought a large parcel of land and fenced it round. He built 3 bungalows of 30 single rooms at one end of the land for rental. After some years, he built two more bungalows of 8 mini flats and was comfortable for a while. But after many years the man, realized he was not getting any younger and active as he used to be. He saw the need to concentrate his finance and effort in other areas, but for his final investment on the land he decided to use the front to build 10 lock-ups shops. He stocked four (4) of them with goods, employed sales girls to manage the stores and rented out the remaining six (6).

He also employed two security men, a gardener, and a caretaker. He engaged the services of plumbers, carpenters and a property agent on contract basis.

The caretaker managed the place, collected rents, paid salary and made accountable returns to the man (the owner who had 100% share of returns on the property). When the man's children were of age, he handed over the management of the property to them. After some time, the devoted and highly skilled caretaker was forced to resign as the man's children employed three caretakers from amongst their friends and cousins: one in charge of the single room bungalow, another in charge of the mini flats and the third in charge of the stores.

The contracts of carpenters and plumbers for maintenance of facilities, were terminated, and a new plumber and a carpenter were employed on a permanent basis, who were of course the children's acquaintances.

It would have been interesting to end the story here to allow you to analyze and predict the future of this man's assets in the face of increasing operating cost, but let's go on.

After some years, poor management resulted in lazy and care-free staff, dilapidated facilities, impromptu collection of rents, theft of some minor assets and accumulated water and light bills, and of course very low returns that never got to the man's hand. The man trying to save his investments started injecting fund for renovation work, maintenance and payment of over-stayed bills. He kept on injecting funds on a continuous basis year in year out; still his financial balance was on the negative side.

PRIVATIZATION!!!

The old man through foresight knew that if the current situation continued he would one day lose all his assets to the effect of bad management by his children. He therefore decided to consult with property managers.

After a crucial discussion, a tight agreement was reached.

Agreement reached and carried out

1. There was an estimation of the total value of the man's assets, outstanding debt owed—electricity and water bills and unpaid rents, payment for service rendered to tenants etc.

2. The above estimate was put into monetary value and sold: 60% of the value went as share to the property managers (core investor). This 60% being the controlling shares gave the new property managers, managerial and technical ownership and control of the entire assets and staff of the property, leaving the man with the remaining 40% as ordinary shares in the property (company) and cash payment for the 60% bought by the property managers.

3. The new managers were free to do anything to the property and the land in order to yield profit, as long as the profit was shared. Part of the profit was injected back into the development of the business to yield more profit and the rest declared as dividend—60% to the care managers, and 40% to the man who still legally had his name as the owner of the property.

4. For the purpose of returning to profitability, the former managers (the man's children) were retired, staff strength reduced to cut cost, redundant and unproductive staff were retired and more money was injected in, to renovate dilapidated structures. All rents owed were recovered, prompt payment restored and all incurred debts paid up.

In the first three years no profit was declared, rather the core managers invested more funds into the business by building a 2 storey building of six three bedroom flats in an empty space on the land. This investment resulted in the employment of more staff.

The men seeing that the core managers were performing creditably well, decided to divert his remaining 40% shares in the property through public offer privatization (POP) to his children, nieces, nephews and any member of his extended family and friends who were interested. He gave his children soft loans to be able to buy the shares.

At the end of the exercise, two members of the man's family were drafted into the board of directors of the property with the firm still bearing the name of the man. In the face of continuous development, the 30-room bungalow was demolished and replaced with a 3-storey building. The property company bought more land for building, made a public offer of right issue to obtain fund to develop a new estate and shopping complex. Returns increased over years.

Looking ahead, the man saw generations getting returns on his investment, many being employed, people having houses to stay, stores and offices to do business and services provided through his investment.

THE MISUNDERSTANDING ABOUT PRIVATIZATION

You may have wondered why this story? I was in the villa when some senior government staff were discussion deregulation of the downstream oil sector an also the forceful resistance put forward by the NLC (Nigerian Labour Congress). Well the floor was open for debate. I was sad when one of the top governmentee lamented; "even the privatization, nobody understands what it can offer the masses, how can you gain from what you do not know about?

I have discovered over time that the solution to the problem of privatization is not just joining the numerous debates on it, but taking advantage of the opportunities it offers.

Where do you fit in? is the question you might ask. Let us cast our minds back to the story. The man can be likened to the government and his children the citizens. From the man's story, you can begin to see why some in the society are against privatization, even when all the factories and companies established by the government have gone under. Most of our parastatals over the years have become drains where government funds flow into with no feedback on the system. They cry out for fund and when it comes, they, like the old man's children squander everything and leave the firm worse off. They later retire to become society's "respected" millionaires.

I don't want to sound too political, but you must realize that the political situation of any country affects the investment climate, and the investment climate affects companies' performances and share price. All this reflects in the economy. An IPO can be under-subscribed if the political climate is rough, because long-term investors may be afraid to invest.

Another point is, you may want to say, "But privatization puts government established parastatals in private hands, won't that jeopardize public interest?"...

No, and even if such companies are hijacked, the new owners intend to make profit and of course pay tax and in making profit, you have to render good product and services to customers and to do that, you must employ competent staff.

So, in summary, first, liberalization takes place followed by privatization, all resulting in competition. And competition brings economic growth, which at the end creates more jobs, and these jobs are given to those who are best capable and enthusiastically deserve them. For example: Nigerian Teleocom. Sector,

- Liberalization:—GSM (MTN, Econet, Global com, Intercellular etc).

- Competition: Global com, Nitel, MTN, Econet etc.

- Privatization: Many stake holders including small-scale investors (SSI).

Folks, leave the debating crowd alone, you must look at where you can fit in, in order to make success in the new scheme of things. Privatization has been described as a national cake but you have to provide the baking ingredients to be a part of the eating.

Privatization is the only way the masses can have a good bite of the national cake. Take a look at the stock market, many former government companies entered the gainers chart, which is a tremendous performance considering that they were totally written off in the past before privatization turned it around.

Privatization, free enterprise and resources control are interrelated and interwoven, as they show the surest way by which this country can move forward.

THE LINK BETWEEN FREE ENTERPRISE AND RESOURCE CONTROL

Now FREE ENTERPRISE allows for a certain degree of resources control. Everyman and woman have to be responsible for managing what is on his/her backyard for meaningful productivity. Every one should be held responsible for their actions and inactions. That is what FREE ENTERPRISE. is all about. But let me kindly point out here that freedom does not mean absence of law, labour or discipline. Now when you are under control, they tell you where to work, what work to do, etc. But under freedom, no one will tell you when to work and you had better start your work early before the night comes when no one can work. Of course, we know the consequences if you don't work at all; no food. So FREE ENTERPRISE and resource control is more difficult to manage and handle that the centrally controlled economy. That is why we talk about the "burdens of freedom." Freedom has its own burdens.

MATURITY BEGINS ON THE DAY WE ACCEPT RESPONSIBILITY FOR OUR OWN ACTIONS."

Lets look at it this way; FREE ENTERPRISE will develop the best of our thinking minds because competition takes the lead and unfair advantages have been removed. And we know that without thinking we can never develop ourselves talk more of our society. Without thinking we will never be able to figure our way out of the slums, we will never discover new things and better ways of doing our work. That is the very essence of FREE ENTERPRISE and that is why it is the only economic system that can save us now.

BREEDING A THINKING GENERATION

It will interest you to know that up till the start of the 18th century, the whole world was at the same level of development. The highest technology then was the hoes and axes we use on our farms. The Europeans, Americans, Africans, Asians and the rest of the world were all using hoes and axes on their farm land. Some where using iron, some gold, some even diamonds to make the hoes and axes.

The most sophisticated weaponry in use at that time was the gun powder. The Kenim Borno Empire of the 17th century around the Lake Chad area of Africa had about thirty musketeers, which means he had the gun powder technology at the time. As a matter of fact, when she was attacked and overpowered by another Empire from Sudan, it was on record that the empire from Sudan had fever soldiers but won the battle because they have move musketeers which implies that they had more powder guns.

In Kano, Northern Nigeria, the Nok culture that dates back to about 900 AD was an iron ore culture. The Ethiopian Empire was as strong and far more advanced than the Roman Empire. That civilization started in Africa (Egypt) is no more news, but what people fail to know is that the civilized Egypt was actually located at the south of Egypt and not Cairo in the North. So it was Southern Egyptians that put the children of Israel in slavery and not the present day Cairo. That is why the Israelites had to go through the sea of Reed popularly known as the Red Sea which is on the south eastern border.

Now the question on my mind is, if the whole world was on the same level of technological development at a certain time how did the rest of the world most importantly the west leave Africa especially, behind in terms of technological development and economic/military advancement. The answer is simply: The west were thinkers." Today I don't support any theory they put forward on why Africa is so backward, we simply refused to put our minds to work.

Today, Africans are still using hoes on their farms while the west have fully mechanized. They have developed the most sophisticated weapons the world have ever witnessed and now they are talking that the next major warfare will be a digital warfare. The Romans Empire and most of the empires of Europe have metamorphosed into powerful self-sufficient countries today like Italy, Germany, Britain, France, and Greece etc. While the Ethiopian empire and the other empires in Africa are now the beds of poverty, hunger, diseases and wars.

A FOOD FOR THOUGHT

What the west did at that time was simple; they were constantly asking them-selves "how can we do this thing or that thing better." Is there a better way of doing a thing, and they followed their thoughts through until they found answers and solution to the problem they aim to solve.

Two illustrations will explain this for us. But first, let me make this point, a recent research showed that only 5% of the world's population is thinking. And among the 5% only 1% followed through their thoughts to a conclusive end. Now, from my understanding, there are two ways of thinking through. One way, are those who have identified a specific problem and hope to solve it someday but meanwhile, they move about on their daily duty normally while they keep an eye for the slightest opportunity that could link up with their search. To these category belongs a man by name Alexander Fleming (1881—1955). Fleming had researched for years on antibacterial substances that would not be harmful to humans but be able to kill the bacteria only. His findings on Penicillin were made at St. Mary's Hospital London. In doing this research, he was breeding (culturing) the bacteria so that he could be able to try a different chemical on them. However, he had a reoccurring problem, whenever there is a fungal growth in his culture, the bacteria don't even sur-vive for him to be able to carry out his test on them with the chemicals.

In 1928, Fleming accidentally rediscovered the long-known ability of peni-cillium fungi to suppress the growth of bacterial cultures but put the finding aside as a curiosity. So, in 1939, principally as an academic exercise, Howard Florey and Ernest Chain undertook an investigation of antibiotics. They pre-pared penicillin and confirmed its remarkable lack of toxicity. When it was first administered to a policeman with multiple infections, there was a dramatic improvement.

Unfortunately though, the manufacture of penicillin (in pathology laboratory) could not keep the pace with requirement (it was extracted from the patient's urine and re-injected), it ran out and the patient later succumbed to infection. Subsequently development amply demonstrated the remarkable therapeutic efficacy of penicillin. And of course, Earnest Bovis Chain (1906—1979) Biochemist, Howard Walter Florey (1898—1969), Professor of Pathology at Oxford University, and Alexander Fleming shared the 1945 Nobel prize for physiology of medicine.

Now when I look back and imagine our world today without a drug like penicillin, this is better not imagined. These men paid the price for us to have a better world today. They were willing to do anything for their discovery to serve humanity. Today people just wake up with an infection that could send them to an early grave and say "give me penicillin." Some think this drug fell from heaven, they didn't just come like that, and people paid the price for generations to enjoy.

(Macfarlane G. 1979, Howard Florey, Oxford) wrote; the importance of this discovery for a nation at war was obvious to these workers but the time, July 1940, was unpropitious, for invasion was feared (During the second world war). The mood of the time is shown by the decision to ensure that, by the time invaders reached Oxford, the essential records and apparatus for making penicillin would have been deliberately destroyed; the productive strain of penicillin mould was to be secretly preserved by several of the principal workers smearing the spores of the mould into the linings of their ordinary clothes where it could remain dormant but alive for years; any member of the tem who escaped (wearing the right clothes) could use it to start the work again. Hm! Survival!

The other set of thinkers are those who will not give their self rest until they see a definite solution to the issue they hope to address—to this group belongs also. From the medical field as an example, a man by name Paul Ehrlich (1854—1915), a German Scientist.

For hundreds of years, moulds have been applied to wounds, but despite the introduction of mercury as a treatment for syphilis (16th century), and the use of Cinchona bark against Malaria (17th century), it was not until the man by name Ehrlich developed modern rational chemotherapy from the idea and observation that aniline dyes selectively stained bacteria in tissue microscopic preparations and could selectively kill them. However, before he got to this point, he had tried different chemical substances on the bacteria and it is on record that he had tried and failed about six hundred times thus giving the name of his final successful discovery the name "Salvarsan 606" which was the first cure for syphilis—According to him, he was searching for that "magic bullet" that can kill the bacteria and not harm the host organism (humans as it were). He says of his discovery "this means......we must learn to aim, learn to aim with chemical substances."

Here we are, Africa! It is annoying that up till now we still don't want to think? By refusing to embrace the free enterprise system, that is exactly what we are saying. Nigeria for one had her golden opportunity in the seventies when she discovered quality oil in large commercial quantities. At that time, Nigeria's leaders were telling the world that her country had so much money that she didn't know what to do with it. The world wasn't shook to wake up and discover at that time that Nigeria was the 10th richest country in the world and had the 3rd highest GDP per capita. Look us now! If we want our children to have a better chance we must start thinking now and we must follow through on our thoughts to a conclusive end.

Free enterprise is the only economic system that can bring about such a thinking culture. Folks, we can't afford any delay, we should hesitate about the power of free enterprise.

ON AFRICA

'Democracy day' is often been celebrated in almost every Africa state these days—after successful democratic elections. Almost every African country now is practicing the democratic system of governance or so they call it, the system has engulfed through African states and is traditionally a showcase of coordinated public spirit. Our democracy day celebration is characterized by class divisions, which gives way to elaborate, egalitarian parades involving millions of people and months of preparation.

But more often than not, this democracy days each time it is been celebrated in any African state has become a reminder of Africa's make-shift democracy, as poverty spread demoralizes masses of people in every nook-and-crony of the streets. Whether elections in most of our countries are free, fair and peacefully coordinated, which should have brought big party, and a fulfilled dream is still a problem to ponder on. To me, it is one more loud warning that to maintain democracy perfectly over the long term, Africa has little choice than to tackle its epic political instability and social inequality, which is one of the worst in the world.

You would agree with me that Africa's fractions and venal political system is usually the last place to look for real leadership on this or any other issue. But these days, alongside images of the severe poverty situation and constant violent eruptions, there's an uncommon sight that even Africa's political leaders apparently can't ignore THE HIV/AIDS epidemic. By most people preferably being silent about what they actually think of when this killer scourge is mentioned, does their gesture reflects, for the moment anyway, a rare sense of unified national purpose in Africa? When president Bush visited, he said the biggest security threat facing Africa is the HIV/AIDS epidemic—not many people took him serious—well I did! We must not deny the potential that this scourge has to wipe out the entire continent. Africa mustn't become a graveyard in our time, and so the responsibility is up to you and me.

Last weeks headlines also included new and old rebel groups rising up with arms against various governments, challenging their authenticity in power and in policies. All this makes it very uneasy to find a suitable position—and even Africa's dysfunctional judiciary and law enforcement agencies have worsened issue. That proper judicial reforms are dearly needed and law enforcement agents should be encouraged and empowered to work effectively and efficiently cannot be over emphasized.

One African leader said after an election "we have to prove we're capable of doing what previous governments couldn't" the biggest challenge to all African leaders who took office through the ballot boxes, is to make democracy system function smoothly and to make these economies—which control a large chunk of the world's economy—work. If they can make that to happen, they'll achieve something even more remarkable: a difficult African system that works.

I believe most of our system that is often touted by the Europeans and American foreign observers can ultimately be improved upon by finding an African "New Deal" that should include everything positive from hunger eradication to underdevelopment and insecurity problems. Even the toughest of critics believe in this mix of ideologies. Agriculture for one needs our concerns. The first step for any meaningful development is food security. The people that cannot feed themselves can't be talking of nuclear physics. It's the food that is in the belly that makes the brain and the body to function. We must first be able to feed ourselves. Create a food reserve and export the excess before we can think of development even in education and economic empowerment in there order of priorities. However, agriculture this days have long outgrown the days of using hoes and cutlasses on our farm lands. It is now capital intensive and a high level of technology and information is needed on every path towards the targeted food security. If we can do this, only thirty percent of the population I believe can achieve our set target and could you imagine what will happen if fifty percent does, go into agriculture?

Well so far, because no one wants the guns to rule anymore, this discipline have won some African leaders an eighty percent approval rating-even though they are yet to score a real achievement. An unexpected applause from the citizenry, where frantic fear of them loosing democracy and the guns coming back which would help slow down foreign investments by more than fifty percent as also aided. "The people in Africa have learned the hard way" says a businessman referring to decades of military rule, dictatorship and economic catastrophes that we are finally saying, "halt"! to.

A lot of us have pledged to adhere to strict democratic principle no matter the cost and apparently set a niche for Africa internationally. One point which is a concern to Africa's economic target is the default on its foreign debt. So many of us are 'sad and disillusioned' by our governments "Did we really borrow and did we really use it"? Someone asked, "Or we just want to be the good little boy for international viewers". We will appreciate every debt relief and forgiveness for sure.

In a welcome development also both top military and police chiefs are radical in their approach to sustaining Africa's fragile systems. They've made it clear, with a somewhat high hand, that military discipline now means not criticizing civilian governments directly. Because it took Africa several years of military rule and wars to get to this stage, says one officer after their joint meetings, "we're more cautions about not flaming out and screwing up again" like so many, previously. So in a closed-door meeting last month, even the civilian leaders and political parties are being careful "we can't fail in any situation" was there verdict.

Perhaps the most important-and most immediate-steps that Africa needs to take is to fully embrace free enterprise system, otherwise known as 'democratic system' if democracy must survive Africa has a millstone public bureaucracy. Its salaries and pensions take a giant share of the nation's gross domestic product respectively. Reining in the corrupt civil service and pension's system, simplifying the countries baroque educational operations and combating massive corruption could help drop poverty rate and free up genuine money at least in the economy. "Africa's macroeconomic approach has been impeccable", says one Eddy man, head of emerging market analysis at New York, noting wryly that the government used to oppose pension's reform. "They understand now that what causes poverty in Africa is the excessive size of the state".

Which ever way, African leaders must realize that what also leaves its over half a billion people in poverty and an estimated fifty-six million on verge of death, is gross inequality. Twenty percent of the population receives eighty percent of the nation's income, while three percent hold almost two-third of the money in the private sector. African leaders will not of course declare a soak-the-rich crusade, but their hesitancy to come out for stiff progressive anti-corruption measure makes their party critics crazy. If only our leaders can bring back part of the funds they looted and re-invest it into African economies, there will be a whole new glorious dimension to the situation back home. We are not saying the looted funds should be sized, we are saying the looters should instead of stockpiling this money in foreign lands, should use it to set up businesses here in Africa, create jobs and improve the economy. One of the biggest reluctance of foreign investors is seeing us coming to keep money with them and in-turn asking them to go and invest their own money in African economy—that's a very complex twist.

More importantly, I believe that people's efforts could waste, unless the inefficiency and indifference of Africa's economic system are re-structured, converting them from 'patronage to rackets political violence' to 'engines of entrepreneurship and economic growth'. Agriculture for one is meant mostly to raise the productive capacity of poor Africans. Also inclusive to insuring that people become producers are religious groups, non-governmental organizations and significantly the private enterprises.

Finally, I feel the real test of our democratic system will stand or fall on these issues, but I won't pinpoint a gauge for success if we can achieve most of our goals on agriculture and rural development, the system will be a success—it would have changed the culture of inequality to some degree. There's no opportunity of change like this in our history.

AFRICA LINKING WITH MODERN INDUSTRIAL CAPITALISM

The last place to look for true leadership no doubt is Africa. Check the state of the countries that some of our past African Leaders have left, it is a crying shame. Usually Leadership in Africa fails before it even begins because it is motivated by personal gains and interest that is all, they don't have the country they rule at heart. Today most of their citizens can't believe their misfortune, tempers are rising everywhere, peoples' patience is fast fading and fingers pointing here and there, but who exactly do we blame.

Most of the wars and poverty in Africa today is primarily as a result of people fighting for what they didn't create. Rebels and terrorist crying peace while they're inflicting pain on the people. Few opportunists come up and decide other men's fate, while claiming power in the name of their gods, preaching words of love and unity but what their actions reflects is an insane scorn. What some of our leaders fail to realize is that you don't solve problem by creating wars and inflicting poverty, hunger, torture and deaths on innocent souls. If we destroy every one around us, then there will be nothing left to defend and protect. Let's stop thinking of the cures and start thinking of ways to prevent.

Maybe they should talk to the Lord and there will be no need for any special revenge! But jokes apart, let Africans and African leaders, past and present stop the phonies and let us live our dreams. Tackling poverty in Africa will need a combination of debt relief, increased aid and most importantly, business and trade initiatives, (that is what Africa can do for itself). To completely enforce blanket trade liberalization policies on poor countries might not be too wise as that leaves them unable to compete with rich producers.

However, Africa must start somewhere to be able to build an Africa for the future. The basic criteria to meet up with the debt relief, developmental and substantial growth is good governance and tackling corruption. For sure the continent has seen many corrupt leaders who have squandered their aid and wealth, but remember that the west had a hand in promoting some of those leaders because it suited them at the time. So if Africa should ask for debt relief and aid today, she is not asking for too much. Only, it is time for all the cash that has been promised to be tackled with actions.

At about a hundred years ago, all of our ancestors were entrepreneurs. Now the number is between 5 and 10 percent. By moving from the farms to the cities, we delegated our freedom to large, centralized organizations. We got soft. We lost our entrepreneurial skills. And now that the new paradigm of the world is changing, we've been forced "back to the farm" so to speak-back to individual responsibility. The whole world is moving away from centralized authority at every kind. With downsizing, companies are splitting into profit teams; smaller PT boats instead of lumbering battleships. Many of those who have been downsized are realizing that being an employee is even riskier than being in business for themselves. That's what is fueling the incredible home-based business revolution of nowadays that home-based business are being created at unprecedented rates.

"THE FUTURE OF PRIVATE ENTERPRISE CAPITALISM IS ALSO THE FUTURE OF A FREE SOCIETY. THERE IS NO POSSIBILITY OF HAVING A POLITICALLY FREE SOCIETY UNLESS THE MAJOR PARTS OF ITS ECONOMIC RESOURCES ARE OPERATED UNDER A CAPITALISTIC PRIVATE ENTERPRISE SYSTEM.

—Milton Friedman

LIVE YOUR DREAM

Many people in Africa today feel as if their lives are worth nothing. They seem to have lost the joy and hope in their living. Do you find yourself in that position? Are you asking yourself if it is possible to build personal wealth in Africa legally and enjoy your success? Yes, it is possible. Africa's hope of an economic revolution will only be possible if you live your dreams.

Living your dreams is not as hard as it may seem. All you need to do is work hard; get the right information, association and the cream. You have to lean strongly on your hopes, it is better to die for what you believe than to live for nothing, so it is all or nothing. Give in your everything. Now is your best chance of your life, so get ready, set and fly high. Learn to wean yourself from the fear of your mind, go for it, it is hit or miss, because it is already too late for you to quit the race of life. So stand up strong go out there and show the world how bad you really want to make a mark on it. Know what to believe, believe the right things and simply bring the heat on it. Get the pace, others will follow. Competition takes the lead. That's it! All eyes on you now so stay and prove a point that you deserve what has been long overdue. Live your dreams and I'll see all my African brothers and sisters at the pinnacle of the world stage. Believe in free enterprise, and embrace free enterprise.

3

"UNDERSTANDING FREE ENTERPRISE"

UNDERSTANDING FREE ENTERPRISE

"OUR DOUBTS ARE TRAITORS AND MAKE US LOSE THE GOOD WE OFT WOULD WIN BY FEARING TO ATTEMPT".

—William Shakespeare

I believe free enterprise offers Africa its surest way of achieving its economic dignity in the nearest future. Free enterprise? Yes! A friend did ask me, "is not free enterprise the economic system that allows a few powerful individuals control the whole large chunk of a country's money?" isn't it a system where there is a free for all fight and the barons, robbers, assassins and powerful cartels have a field day? Doesn't this system allow people to be involved in all sorts of abuses like child labour and girls trafficking? If everybody begins to build factories there is bound to be great environmental pollution with really no one to check it. A system where all the wealth in a country is circulating in the hands of a few prominent citizens—have been all the comments you would likely hear about free enterprise.

The truth is without free enterprise there wouldn't be freedom and democracy, with all their benefits of liberalization, deregulation and private ownership would be null and void. No doubt, free enterprise is an important subject today, but while the rest of the world is rushing to embrace it, Africa that needs it the most to accelerate its economic misfortune so as to catch up with the developed world has still not come to light about what it's all about. Africa is still focused on war, poverty and failures, worse still, many of our own people don't even know how free enterprise works or how the system can help them make a better living and a better life.

Sometimes, I still wonder why some of our academicians, social activist and labour unions leaders forget or refuse to acknowledge the incredible strengths and successes of free enterprise? Why do they cling to outdated notions about government and centrally controlled economy when it is now evident that the promises made by those economic systems do not hold?

Even though free enterprise has its shortcomings, some recurring failures in the past have made this clear; however we all ought to seek ways of avoiding those pit-falls in the future. Inspite of those pit-falls, free enterprise has become the world's economic system of choice, and it is easy to understand why. Although I do not want you to believe that it's just all about copying the American system that has been of tremendous success and also very beneficial to its citizens. But we could see that it has also benefited the rest of the world and that's why millions of immigrants are struggling to get to that God's own country especially from this part of our world. No doubt, the story of America's free enterprise success is a good example of the power of free enterprise at work.

Nigeria for one has experienced many unpleasant ordeals under government-controlled economy. NEPA, NITEL and REFINERIES are all part of the businesses, which has failed to be productive and match emerging responsibilities. These businesses could not function effectively and efficiently for over two decades now, what on earth makes you think it can function overnight if they are still under the same management of government. Everyday it becomes clearer and clearer that they are even depreciating the more some look like though they have defied all possible solutions but just put these businesses in the hands of private owners who have invested into it and see if they will allow their investment waste or yield returns!

That is why when I listen to the critics of free enterprise and privatization, I ignore it altogether. Because if we keep listening to them our lives will remain stagnant and begin to depreciate afterwards in terms of self worth and personal success.

I'm not trying to side those who want to impose on us completely the western system, NO! We sure have different cultures and peculiarities, but no doubt at all, America's way of private ownership and free enterprise is the best way. America is a nation that was built on private ownership and free enterprise; I say this to anyone who cares to listen. Free enterprise is not perfect, but it is the only way to take this country to its highest potential.

WE NEED TO MAKE A BETTER STANDARD OF LIVING

People want to live in a country where they are free to try new solutions, to trade and do business without restrictions, to compete in a free market place, to choose careers, and to own their own businesses. People want to experience the joy of free enterprise, that's why they want to live in America. If we are convinced that democracy and free enterprise are the world's only economic hope, why wouldn't we want to share in its benefits? People should be free to participate in a free-market economy and to liberate a whole new generation of entrepreneurs.

When the global system for mobile communication (G.S.M) hit Africa, and Nigeria's president Obasanjo had the courage to bull doze the monopoly and walls the government had built around that sector of the economy, private telecom companies entered Nigeria. And then some erupted from within Nigeria to give some competitions. Now several thousands of excited citizens, determined, committed men and women have their own businesses. They, too, are discovering how free enterprise in action can help overcome years of poverty and despair.

Don't misunderstand me; this free enterprise is not just about making money. Of course people want financial independence for themselves and there family. Why shouldn't they anyway? But they want something even more spectacular, true freedom to be who they really want to be socially, phys-ically, psychologically, mentally and emotionally. They want deeper satisfac-tion. Not just financial freedom, but freedom of the spirit. The freedom to become complete and total person. The freedom to be what God wants us to be. The freedom of mind and imagination that can only exist in a truly demo-cratic society. The freedom not just to survive but to find genuine satisfaction in life.

What we think of people matter in the success of free enterprise system. If we think of them as children of God, possessing a divine spark and having God-given worth, it follows that we ought to treat all people with respect and dignity. But if we think of people in a strictly material sense, devoid of any spirituality and gaining worth only through the government or state, then what happens? Look at communist history to answer that question.

And what we think of the nature and resources of the earth is also crucial to the decision we make about our use of this wonderful resources. If we think of this amazing continent and all her treasures as God's gifts to us, of ourselves as God's appointed caretakers of these priceless resources, then it follows that we will love and care for the continent.

WHAT IS FREE ENTERPRISE SYSTEM

Although perhaps not perfect in all respects, capitalism upholds free enterprise, and free enterprise offers the creative individual far move opportunities than any other economic system. No other system allows the individual to make as much money for his or her talent, service and creative ideas. Totally free economics offer the enterprising individual unlimited potentials. A free market place operates on supply and demand and encourages and rewards the industrious. Any system that does not reward incentive and places too much emphasis on poverty is in danger of decline and fall into a state of national poverty.

I buy the idea of humanistic programs that aid the mentally and physically handicapped; they really deserve every body's support. But any able-bodied person who refuses to work does not need help. The bible puts it clear, "Anyone who will not work should not eat". It is my belief that rather than help, many of our socialistic programs (people bank, FSP, FEAP, NAPEP etc) are robbing those they propose to help by taking away both their incentive and dignity, thereby promoting a state of financial bondage. Lack is a state of mind first; then it's expressed by restricted living. To reward poverty-thinking in able-bodied individuals is, in my concept f self-reliance, counter-productive to the individuals concerned and society in general. I believe great value should be put on self-reliance, and unrestricted rewards should be available to the producers. Research has shown that the greater the perceived value to an individual, the more creative and dedicated will be his effort to obtain it. Society as a whole advances through the efforts of creative goal oriented, individually successful persons. Successful individuals create a successful society.

Any notion that the captains of industry—business people are unethical or not worthy of trust is totally erroneous. Yes, some businessmen do believe in taking unfair advantage of the public. Such unaware, greedy types are definitely among us. But is this good reason to fault the entire system? I think not! Crooks are crooks, be they dressed in babariga or business suits, engaged in "white collar" crimes with per and paper or be they wearing black jeans, using a knife or gun to rob someone. Neither lawless group represents the morals or beliefs of our free enterprise system. Both should be vigorously prosecuted!

My readers would say that I'm an advocate of free market economics. Honestly I am. I do believe that we can achieve both our financial and national freedom with it. Our economies can become the best. I still think African countries are lands of great opportunities. Anyone can become very rich in our great countries. I personally also believe that as a person decides to enjoy personal wealth; it is also beneficial that he become active to enhance and uphold a system that makes personal wealth so easily obtainable.

HOW WILL FREE ENTERPRISE WORK IN OUR SOCIETY

The thing that is most responsible for growth in any enterprise is sales and marketing of product or services. When business enterprises are in the hands of government, workers are not motivated to work. Independent ownership and its life-long advantages fires enthusiasm, loyalty and commitment in the heart of millions of independent business people around the world.

The main reason why all the enterprises in the hands of the government fail woefully is simply because of this: people are not motivated to get the job done. They couldn't own their own piece of the business resources; they don't even own the tools with which they worked with. As a result, they don't even care to take good care of what ever was entrusted into their hands. They feel everything should be paid for by the state including the responsibility of the inefficiency and decay of these enterprises.

That's why I have decided to lend my voice by traveling across this country, speaking out for free enterprise and its reward of recognition and hope and freedom. In free enterprise, the individual is free to own the resources and the tools necessary to his business. And in so doing the individual himself is free.

When we look carefully back, every time the government took control of a business or enterprise, productivity decreases. And every time the government gave back to the people the rights of ownership, productivity increases. The reason is clear: Most of us parents who have teenage kids at home driving our cars would have notice that, the kids don't care about the state of the car because they aren't the one's who buy the fuel for the car or the regular servicing of the car. If the car develops a problem, they just come back home and park it. The problem could even be a simple tyre-fix, but no they just don't give a damn. But try this if you've not, immediately ownership of that car is turned to them, suddenly, you would see the responsible way that same car will be taken care of. Somewhere along the line they learned the freedom and the responsibility of ownership.

Whenever private individuals own a business two things happen; they last longer and they are used much more effectively. That's why the American farmer who owns the land and the tractor on it keeps the land groomed and the tractor too always in good condition throughout till harvest. He puts lights on his tractor and works through the night, and as a result, that farmer receives greater and greater rewards for a job efficiently done.

No doubt for sure, even when I try to help and explain how free enterprise works, I still strongly believe that privatization and deregulation is the key formula for our nation's future. However, the secret to real lasting success of free enterprise and business is love and compassion. That is why when I talk these days I more often than not, include love and compassion to every package of my presentations. We must let love guide us at every stage on our road to acquiring wealth and in the use of that wealth. People think I'm mad when I say love, not profit, is the ultimate goal of free enterprise. Say it anyway you want, but know this, when love inspires and informs free enterprise, profit follows, the quality of human life is advanced, and the nation is restored and renewed. When love is not an active ingredient in the process, profits may follow temporarily, but the long-term cost in human suffering and in the depletion of the nation is far more than we dare to pay.

At the later part of this book, I have tried to explain this vision of free enterprise being properly mixed with love, which has captured my entrepreneurial spirit and which directs and confronts me every business day. And I believe also that as we peep into the lives of businessmen and women across the globe, whose ideas about free enterprise has informed and inspired me, it will do the same for you as well.

Right now I think it is convincing to say that free enterprise has become the world's economic system of choice because it grants people everywhere the freedom to dream about making a profit (the money we have left after paying all our bills) and the means to see those dreams come true. Free enterprise isn't great because it allows a handful of people to make billions. It is great because it allows millions of people to become what they want to be.

"WHERE LOVE IS, THERE GOD IS"

Regrettably, there have always been (and will always be) greedy, ruthless, uncaring capitalists who think it's right to make a profit even if that process leads to the suffering of people and to the destruction of our nation. Honest and compassionate capitalists still want to make a profit, but they are determined that real profits come when the good of people and the planet comes first.

Profit made at the expense of human or national suffering is not a profit at all. The real costs are not being figured in. those bottom lines should not be even written in black, but in blood red. "Profits" that demeans and dehumanizes our brothers and sisters or depletes and destroys the nation will lead eventually to the death of us all as surely as the wish of Adolph Hitler to turn the world under his power led to the destruction of his dreams and to the death of those he loved most.

Mixing love with free enterprise distinguishes real profit from fool's gold. It cares about setting people free to dream for themselves and for the nation, and then gives them the means to see that their dreams come true.

As I earlier said, in the following pages, I will use stories from inside and outside Nigerian businesses and inform the principles of free enterprise, as I understand them. To tell these stories, I am taking something of a risk. First and foremost because so many books have chronicled the lives of those who lived the stories, many of us like me could have read them all and even tell them so much better. And secondly, because there are so many Nigerians and Africans whose stories are equally moving, but I just didn't have the opportunity to hear them and include them. Remember, however, even if your story is not told now if you keep faith with free enterprise, you will eventually become a gold fish which has no hiding place and destiny will always include you in its hall of fame as those who set-out the legacy of a free system.

BENEFITS OF FREE ENTERPRISE

In the 1920's, the famous American lawyer Clarence Darrow was approached by a female client whose legal problems he has solved. "How can I ever show my appreciation, Mr. Darrow?" She asked. "Ever since the Phoenicians invented money," Darrow replied. "There has been only one answer to that question".

I believe in free enterprise because it provides us and Africa one great hope of economic recovery. It is undoubtedly the determining factor of our financial future. If even you get a job at all, will you spend your lifetime working at a job you don't like? The surest way to find out what free enterprise is all about is to try it yourself. The good thing about free enterprise is that you can make it easier and quicker for yourself, spend more time reading the history of free enterprise and stories of courageous men and women who led the way.

You will see the need for this when you look at the economic mess Africa has put herself in. clearly we need some directions and guidelines, and we need them fast. If we look at the history of free enterprise, it will help us understand the rules of the game and understanding the rules makes playing the fame successfully much more easily. Understanding how the system works will save millions of people their financial dreams.

There are three major economic systems:

1. Free Economy or Democratic Economy:—This is a system where the individuals run the economy. It's what is also known as free enterprise or free market system or capitalism.

2. Planned Economy:—This is the system where everything is put in the hands of the government. That is the state run the economy.

3. Mixed Economy:—In this system, both the government and individuals run the economy. It is what is being practiced in most African countries including Nigeria, and we are saying it doesn't fit anymore.

We want African countries to shift from the Mixed Economic System to the Free Economic System. Though most countries are moving towards free enterprise gradually, we are saying, "move completely", "move now".

The main components of free enterprise are:-

1. Private ownership of wealth and freedom to do so.

2. Freedom of enterprise, that is, free to use wealth.

So if you own anything; a home, a car, some money, a phone, a computer, working tools, stocks, bonds, shares, a pen and paper etc, you are already practicing free enterprise. So I won't be wrong to say that everyone can be a free enterpriser. (Another name for free enterprise is capitalism).

I suppose that one of the reasons I tended toward using free enterprise, as a less inflammatory way of describing the great economic system of America which we so much admire is because of the spark of entrepreneurship it ignites in the life of the children of this world. So let's do everything in our power to bring it burning to African kids. When any little kid buys a thing for one naira and sells same for one naira fifty kobo with the fifty kobo as profit, that kid should be praised and encouraged for his/her creativity and labour. Were you ones that little kid years ago with a tray of vegetable stand? Feel again that spirit of free enterprise that you felt then. Dare to dream those old dreams again. "There is no security in this life, there is only opportunity", says General Douglas. What would you like to do with the rest of your life? Do it! Take the first step today and everything else will follow.

Somewhere down inside of you, I know your own entrepreneurial spirit is struggling to be free. Don't be afraid to try. Go for it. The journey begins with that first step. Find a company of friends who will help you see your dreams come true. And one day you will know that the real joy of free enterprise is not just finding your own personal fulfillment and financial security. The real joy is helping other people to find personal fulfillment and financial security for themselves.

WEALTH OF NATIONS

The ideas that shaped free enterprise which is also the same ideas that have helped all successful business people came from a Scottish man called Adam Smith. He is the father of free enterprise and author of the world's classic 'Wealth of Nations'. Adam Smith was a great thinker and had a great character.

Smith was born in 1723 in a little Scottish seaport named Kirkcaldy, near Edinburgh. He entered the University of Glasgow at the age of fourteen and then won a scholarship to Oxford University, where he spent an additional two years. After Oxford, he was appointed to the faculty at the University of Glasgow.

While still a teenager, Smith began to ponder this question: Why are some nations richer than others, and how do these richer nations produce more to eat, wear, and use than the others? His answer to this question led the world to the development of the free-enterprise system. A nations wealth was not increased by the accumulation of money, said Smith, but by the division of labour.

The world was about to learn that the energy, ideas and skill all waiting to be discovered in millions of people were more valuable than gold. To paraphrase Smith: the division of labour is the main cause of the increase in public wealth because a nation's wealth is in proportion to the different creative abilities of people and not the quantity of gold.

What exactly does this mean? You can find Smith's ideas in his 'Wealth of Nations', without a doubt the most famous and influential book on economics ever published. At the beginning of that book Smith told a story to illustrate what he meant by the division of labour.

The subject of this celebrated story is a pin. The story goes somewhat like this. A person not trained to be a pin maker—by working very diligently and carefully—succeed in making one pin per day, from scratch. At the most, a person with some experience might make twenty. But even in Smith's day the pin business didn't work that way.

A pin manufacturer was typically made up of workers who specialized in certain tasks. In Smiths illustration, one person might make the wire, a second person straighten it, a third cut it to length, a fourth sharpen one end, and a fifth prepare the other end to receive the head. Another two or three people might be involved in fabricating and installing the head. A typical pin might be the result of many individual workers, each with a specific task to do. In the 1700s, a small company with ten workers could turn out 48,000 pins a day. That's 4,800 each. But if every worker made pins separately, the factory might make as few as 10 or at the most 200.

Smiths little story clearly illustrates his point. When the labour necessary to complete a task or make a product is divided into specific, distinct operations, productivity soars. When it does, a nation's wealth is increased. But that's not all—when workers specialize, they learn to solve problems better, and the more likely it is that they will invent machines that can help increase productivity. In other words, the division of labour is also a key factor in the development of new technology.

In two words: People matter. They have a variety of gifts to contribute to the manufacturing process. Free them to develop and exercise those gifts. Smith's insight was fundamental and it made sense of a complex system that people really didn't understand very well. But his insight didn't stop with pin factories. He had a lot more to say, not only about nations and their economies, but about people and their importance to the economic process.

Smith was curious about how people made economic decisions. This was a result of his puzzling over how they made moral decisions. Like most serious-minded people in his days, Smith started out studying for the ministry. He didn't plan to be an economist in fact, in those days there weren't any economists. When Adam Smith got interested in what we would now call the study of economics and psychology, he pursued a major they called "moral philosophy".

THE INVISIBLE HAND THEORY

Adam Smith had a theory about how economics and psychology work together in the market place. It's called the theory of the invisible hand. Smith was concerned with how people could make good moral judgments in the face of powerful, conflicting motives like self-interest and self-preservation. Also, he was also concerned with how people make good economic judgments under the same kind of pressures.

He argued that people do the right thing-most of the time because each of them possesses an "inner person" who plays the role of an "impartial spectator" who approves or disapproves their actions. Smith considered this impartial spectator to be a powerful voice-a sort of loud-spoken conscience—that is tough to ignore. He saw people driven by their passions, but self-regulated by their ability to reason and their uniquely human capacity for compassion.

What's more, self-seeking people are often led by an invisible hand-without knowing it or intending it—to advance the interest of society. In the economic arena, as opposed to the moral arena, he substituted for the impartial spectator another regulating force: competition. In a free marketplace, a person's passion to get ahead is kept under control by competition.

COMPETITION

Smith considered the competitive urge to be a basic part of human nature. And this is not a crime, because it is turned into a socially beneficial force if it is allowed free expression. Why? Because in pitting one person's self-interest against another's, the invisible hand comes into play. The invisible hand influences what products will be produced and at what price. Smith argued that the invisible hand is a powerful force in ensuring that society gets the products it wants it a price it's willing to pay.

Smith believed that society should give free reign to everyone's desire to get ahead—to compete. Above all, he said, the government should not try to legislate goodness or generosity. People are much more likely to do the right thing if they can see some personal advantage to it. He believed strongly in economic incentive.

FREE MARKET PLACE

Smith had a well-developed conscience and a low tolerance for exploitive business practices. He was not naïve, nor was he blind to the greedy practices of some merchants and manufacturers in his day. In fact, he said once that when people in the same trade get together, even for a party, the conversation always seemed to turn into a conspiracy to cheat the public. Still, he believed that the power of the invisible hand would over-power "devilish pacts" concocted by business people who were dishonest.

When businesses did make exorbitant profits, Smith usually looked to see whether government was playing a role in supporting them with some kind of law or regulation. According to him, greedy business people often looked to the government for help in maintaining their position. The government was in a position to render the invisible hand ineffective. The government could impose restrictions on trade, grant monopolies to some industries, or favour others with protective laws.

Smith did not believe that anyone should have special privileges. If businesses gave themselves preferential privileges by conspiring, together, or if government granted them legislative favours or interfered in anyway with competition, then the invisible hand could not work. It had to work in a context of "natural liberty". In which everyone's best interests were served. But the government had to stay out of business and vice versa. It's another Adam Smith idea we need to rediscover and rediscover fast.

Smith particularly feared unholy alliances between business and government should not, he said, heed "the mean rapacity, the monopolizing spirit of merchants and manufacturers, who neither are, nor ought to be, rulers of mankind". Smith was realistic about human nature and idealistic about the necessity for the exercise of conscience in the marketplace.

LAISSEZ—FAIRE

Smith advocated a policy of laissez-faire, meaning literally, "allow to act". In other words, n economic matters you ought to leave well enough alone. His economic philosophy was based on he assumption that the invisible hand would guide peoples businesses—entire industries—with impartial efficiency, only if they were left alone. But in the absence of government interference, how does it help us prevent runaway greed?

Let's say a powerful businessman has developed a food product that is a big hit at the Kaduna Polytechnic, say plantain chips. Or, as the businessman decides to call them, Pringles. Suppose the students at Kaduna Polytechnic develop a craving for Pringles and buy out his entire supply every afternoon. But the businessman—because he is both powerful and greedy—decides he doesn't want to go to the trouble of making enough of these plantain chips to meet demand. So he starts charging more for those he makes. A lot more. He's the only one making the product, so he can charge what he wants.

Along comes another creative young woman, she may be poor and powerless, but she notices that this greedy businessman is making a lot of money charging high prices for something that's not hard to make. What's going to happen? Competition. She is going to give that businessman a run for his money. And do you think she's going to charge more or less than the greedy businessman? Less, of course. This new competitor wants the student business. So, as Smith might say, a man who lets his greed gets out of control is soon going to find his competitors taking his business away.

Now about that laissez-faire issue. What if the Director of Kaduna Poly decides that only one businessperson can sell plantain chips? Pringles became the official chips of Kaduna Poly and the other young woman's product, is banned. There could be a lot of different reasons for the Director to limit sales to one businessperson. Maybe he's concerned that the pavement in front of Kaduna Poly is getting too crowded with businesses and kiosk blocking the entrance. Or maybe the greedy businessman is a personal friend.

Whatever the motivation—safety, favoritism, altruism—the result will probably be the same, higher prices. One thing to remember about the invisible hand is this: it doesn't matter whether interference in the marketplace is for good reasons or bad, the effect is identical. In Smiths view, the invisible hand is indifferent to moral issue—it is completely unbiased. Smith believed that people have to make their own moral choices. Any attempt to legislate goodwill in the marketplace is doomed to failure. Self-interest is just too powerful, and the only thing that can contain it is competition.

The age of free enterprise really began after the publication of 'The Wealth of Nations'. Smith provided a rational basis—a way of thinking that was a conceptual breakthrough. Up until this time, people hadn't always thought of themselves individual agents, free to make decisions on their own. They thought of themselves as members of a community or class. With the old way of thinking, decisions were made by consensus or fiat, and the individual didn't count for much. In the world before Galileo, events often seemed to happen for mysterious, unknown reason. The world seemed to be a chaotic place. If someone was wealthy, or acquired wealth, it was because God ordained it.

How economics functioned—the process by which wealth was accumulated or acquired—was not understood. Because of this people were willing to accept poorly formulated religious explanations, which had little or nothing to do with the truth. The poor simply accepted their economic status as God's will. The powerful claimed God's authority for their carefully guarded special privileges. These explanations were seldom more than rationalized excuses for the status quo.

The idea that it is honourable to be motivated by profit—the concept that work might be a means to an end, and not the end itself—is relatively new. Society and the faith used to condemn the profit motive as sinful and wrong.

Smith put things together in a brilliantly simple and powerful concept built around self-interest. While smith was an advocate of laissez-faire he opposed policies of legislating morality, he was also an advocate of the highest personal standards of morality and conduct. He did not turn a blind eye to corruption or greed. It would be a mistake to use Smith's ideas as a way to rationalize or excuse those who abuse the free enterprise system. Conscience was at the center of his concern. He assumed that people had inside them an urge to do the right thing—an inner voice. And upon that assumption free enterprise was based.

STRATEGIES TO FREE ENTERPRISE

Guided by Adam Smith's principles, free enterprise has produced the greatest prosperity the world has ever known. There have been failures though; Karl Marx was just one of the critics of free enterprise who made that very clear. We all know that there will always be greedy capitalist, girls trafficking, child labour exploiters and robber barons. Nevertheless, these are the exceptions and not the rules. Free enterprise remains the only economic system that gives us hope that we can pull our nations and their people back from the brink of poverty and push them straight into an age of prosperity and peace.

'The Wealth of Nations' understands free enterprise and the principles that make it work. Learn it from Adam Smith or learn it the hard way.

1. If you want to succeed in business, liberate other people's gifts.

2. Serve other people's needs and you'll find your own needs being met.

3. Be glad for competition. It makes the system work.

4. The profit motive is good. Accumulating wealth is necessary for a business to succeed and for a nation's people to prosper.

5. Understand and respect each individual's conflict between self-interest and conscience. Always balance both your business practices and your own heart.

6. After the government ensures all people's basic rights to life, liberty, and the pursuit of happiness, encourages politicians to stay out of the business of business.

7. Don't be scared when other countries begin to compete. Learn from their success. Work harder. Don't ask for favours. Pull down the walls government would build between such.

8. Give everybody an equal chance regardless of tribe, creed, sex, faith or colour.

9. Always remember, human-beings welfare is the ultimate goal of economic activity. It doesn't matter how little or how much gold is in treasury if people's needs are not met!

Well, that's looking back. Let's look to the future. Adam Smith developed those principles in the not so ancient past. How can we use them to help guide us into our near future? Read and digest them, ask yourself what will happen to me and to my family if I rediscovered these old principles and put them to work in my own life and business? What could happen to our nations poised on the brink of economic bankruptcy if we all rediscovered these principles and let them guide us in the future? And what will happen if we don't?

Well I am not just talking like a really good preacher. I believe in the future of Africa. This is the greatest moment our African nations have ever known. There has never been a better opportunity to succeed in business, to see our financial dreams come true. Let's go for it. The principles by which free enterprise is built have been tasted and trusted in so many great nations in the past. Let us embrace and trust it to guide our nations to their desired future.

When you work hard and still can't afford the basic necessities of life, you begin to feel helpless and angry. Free enterprise gives people the chance to get ahead. When they can earn enough money to afford their basic necessities and even see some of their dreams come true by so doing, their sense of helplessness and anger is replaced by feelings of hope and self-worth.

It will be much more better for most of us if very early in life we realize that free enterprise is the only sure way to financial independence. When we talk of free enterprise most people don't believe it's for them. They think free enterprise is for the rich, maybe middle class men with university degree or those folks with daddy's large cash in the bank. Because they are poor and feel disadvantaged academically or even physically, they assume there is no room for them. They can't believe in the privatization programs of this country or the deregulation and commercialization of the various sectors. They don't trust anything the authority does that is inclined towards taking us to the point of the free enterprise system, because they don't think there is liberty and justice for all. It's surprising that the government is the one pushing for free enterprise when in real sense the public should, what an irony. We should be telling the government to privatize and not the other way round. Maybe most people don't really understand the whole concept of free economy. I just found myself being on the side of the government on this issue, I'm not comfortable at all, if you are holding this book in your hands right now, I only ask you for one thing; that you produce, and free enterprise will surely reward you on the same scale and by the same rules that it rewarded all other great business people we've known in history.

My heart goes for all the young people across this country that have hoped and dreamed of the promises of Adam Smith's free enterprise theory. It's true that sometimes living out our dreams is not as easy as it's made to sound but you have to be strong or else you will see shame. We cannot afford to waste another life. The rules must be fair; the same opportunity must be given to everyone. Let the best be on the top, let merit put them on the right seat. Let reward be given based on creativity. Free enterprise has proven to do just that, especially when we refuse to let tribe, religion, gender, physical limits, or anything else stands in the way. I can see the tears of determination in the eyes of many who want to pledge allegiance to this system, the country's flag and Africa as a whole for what they really want to be.

BECOME AN ADVOCATE OF FREE ENTERPRISE

After all said and done, I believe that practicing free enterprise is the secret of real financial success.

"EVERYTHING I DO, I DO FOR PROFIT"

—H.L. Hunt.

We have more than not, heard of compounding interest. Let's look at this practical example and then take your choice. You are given two employment offers. Both will last only one month and one week, a total of 37 days!

No 1 offer will bring you one thousand naira (N1, 000) a day for 37 days.
No 2 offer is one kobo (1K) the first day and double that amount each day until the 37 days are up.

Here are the results:

DAY	OFFER NO 1 NAIRA N	OFFER NO 2 (NAIRA) N
1	1000	.01
2	1000	.02
3	1000	.04
4	1000	.08
5	1000	.16
6	1000	.32
7	1000	.64
8	1000	1.28
9	1000	2.55
10	1000	5.10
11	1000	10.20
12	1000	20.40
13	1000	40.80
14	1000	81.60
15	1000	163.20

16	1000	326.40
17	1000	650.00
18	1000	1,300.00
19	1000	2,600.00
20	1000	5,200.00
21	1000	10,400.00
22	1000	20,800.00
23	1000	41,600.00
24	1000	83,200.00
25	1000	165,750.00
26	1000	331,500.00
27	1000	663,000.00
28	1000	1,326,000.00
29	1000	2,652,000.00
30	1000	5,304.000.00
31	1000	10,608,000.00
32	1000	21,216,000.00
33	1000	42,432,000.00
34	1000	84,864,000.00
35	1000	169,728,000.00
36	1000	339,456,000.00
37	1000	678,912,000.00
Total	37,000	678,912,000.00

Offer No 1 would bring you a nice N37,000 for 37 days, now consider offer No 2—double-your-money pyramiding in just 37 days, starting with a lowly penny would bring you SIX HUNDRED AND SEVENTY-EIGHT MIL-LION, NINE HUNDRED AND TWELVE THOUSAND NAIRA! A fabulous fortune!!! That amount of money may not seem realistic to you, but the concept of money-making money is 100% valid! Especially when you have 365 ¼ days at your disposal.

I just want us to see that right from the beginning of time, real opportunities avail itself to us all but many people have missed out to have made their fortune. Simply compounding interest could have been done it for anyone with foresight and financial planning. Anybody could have made wealth in this world and enjoyed what the Bill Gates of the world are enjoying-fame, prestige, status and respect.

Many a times most of us have dreamed of a better life for ourselves and our family and even our generation. We get worried about our future, wondering if we would spend the whole of our lives never having enough, working long tedious hours in jobs our parents worked and came out empty handed.

Though many workers don't want to feel ungrateful, but deep down they know that the salary at their jobs is just too small. Some could hardly afford to pay the kid's school fees and so those kids will end as primary-school drop-outs, at most still secondary school so like their parents and grandparents before them, they would spend their adult lives doing the same jobs for the meager salary paid in the footsteps of their fathers. This is a very common phenomenon here in the northern part of Nigeria were I grew up. For sure some degree of free enterprise exist in Nigeria, but most of our lives and the lives of those we love had not been touched by its benefits. So the question is, is free enterprise system failing? If not, how can it affect our lives? Here is the answer.

THE NEED FOR LOVE AND COMPASSION IN FREE ENTERPRISE SYSTEM

"LEADERSHIP IS NOT JUST ABOUT POWER, STRENGTH, COURAGE, EFFICIENCY AND EFFECTIVENESS BUT IT IS

ABOUT COMPASSION, DIALOGUE, VISION, MOBILIZATION AND SPIRITUALITY".

—President Obasanjo.

Some argue that compassion is directly opposed to profit—making and that it actually distorts serious business and causes trouble for everyone. They are not running a charitable organization like mother Theresa they say, they are running a business enterprise. But the truth is that, love and compassion is that very vital ingredient that makes the free enterprise system successful both for the business owner and the worker alike. Love and compassion needs to be in every-bodies heart.

The dictionary defines compassion as "a feeling of deep sympathy for another's suffering or misfortune, accompanied by a desire to alleviate the pain or remove its cause". Doing something you feel obligated to do is not bad; it just isn't the same as compassion. Real compassion involves our whole being. It means to feel sorry about someone or something and to act with passion to help end the suffering and even alleviate it's cense. A compassionate act comes out of a compassionate feeling. Compassion is feeling and acting together. Why is it then that some people care about other's feelings and sufferings to act compassionately while some don't care at all?

The human's mind and heart is always at war between two dominant forces. The forces of God and the forces of Satan. The forces of Satan lead to sin and eventually death. While the forces of God leads to peace and abundant life. The characteristics of Satan's call and obedience are: promptings of evil towards self-centeredness, indifference, hatred, greed, lust, jealousy, murder, immorality, and all forms of evil rituals. While the characteristics of the call of God and obedience to His call are: peace, gentleness, humbleness, generosity, kindness, faith, hope, good deeds and above all is love. Love is so important that it is the center of Jesus' teachings in founding the faith of Christianity. In fact when ask what was the greatest commandment, He replied with these words: "thou shall love the Lord your God with all your heart, with thy entire mind and with all thy soul" for this is the first and the greatest commandment. And He went further to add that "the second is like the first, thou shall love thy neighbour as thy-self." In His declaration of the final judgment, He made it clear that the good people shall be rewarded for acting with compassion towards the hungry, thirsty, naked, sick, stranger and people in prison. He said "if you have done it unto one of the least people, you have done it to me".

Mohammed, the Islamic religious prophet in the seventh century Jesus, also saw the human life as a struggle between good and evil. He thought His followers that one's goal is to submit to the will of God in the war against evil. Alleviating suffering and helping the needy was an integral part of Mohammed's teachings. He taught them that praying and other religious acts were worthless and hypocritical in the absence of active service to the needy. As a matter of fact, in the Koran, the prophet writes: "Man is by nature timid, when evil befalls him, he panics, but when good things come to him, he prevents them from reaching others". It is Satan who whispers, "Keep it". It is God, who replies, "Give it to the poor", in exchange for "noble sacrifice" God promises prosperity.

I don't know which religion or school of taught you belong, but what I know as a Christian is that "if you have no love, you are nothing". We all know frankly speaking that all of our religions have over the years cause question to be ask because of how some have been starved, tortured, killed and even enslaved by the misuse and misunderstanding of these religions. Though that is not enough reason to keep us from affirming the compassion that they preach.

I believe that love and compassion is the only foundation on which we can build a business or rebuild Africa's shattered economies. If we are to find a way out of the current economic chaos, we must learn to love this continent and its people as they have never been loved before. Love and freedom are inseparable brothers. William Hazlitt said that the 'love of liberty is the love of others". George Bernard Shaw said that liberty means responsibility—that's why most people dread it. Jesus said, "Greater love has no man than this, that he gives up his life for his friend". Compassion means, according to Rich Devos, "taking responsibility for the people and the planet no matter what the cost".

THE LEGACY OF LOVE AND COMPASSION

In spite of all odds and attempts to resist it, compassion has struggled to find it's way through in every culture and people right from when the world began. Right from those days, the ancient Jewish people put aside 10% (a tithe) of every harvest to support their religious faith and to care for their poor. Also, a corner of every farming field was not to be harvested so that the poor could glean what remained to support themselves. In fact, every seventh year the fields were left unplanted to rest the soil and allow the poor to gather whatever crops might grow up from the previous years' plantings.

The spirit of compassion that guided good king Asoka can be summarized in his own words: "All men are my children, as for my own children I desire that they be provided with all the welfare and happiness of this world and of the next, so I desire for all men as well".

The teachings of Jesus and His followers are centered upon loving our neighbours as we love ourselves. Time and time again Jesus returned to his familiar theme: feeding the hungry, clothing the naked, healing the sick, and confronting the dying. Shortly after His death and resurrection, the early Christians began to collect church funds through voluntary offerings. Deacons were elected to use these funds to care for widows, orphans, and others in need.

In later years the churches were organized into districts, each with its own hospital, an alms office for collecting and dispensing donations, an orphanage, and a shelter for babies who were unwanted or whose parents were too poor to give them the necessary care. The word hospital comes from the French—hotel Dieu or God's hotel. It was not really a hospital, as we know it, but a place of refuge for the poor and of hospitality for strangers.

Modern hospitals have their roots in early Christian charity. They began as rooms in the house of a bishop set aside where the sick and dying could be cared for, usually by the bishop himself. The first documented hospital on record was established at Caesaree in A.D. 369 by St. Basil. According to one historian, "it was a veritable city, with pavilions for various diseases and residences for physicians, nurses and convalescents. St. Gregory called it a "heaven on earth".

Well now lets look at even more modern examples lets consider the story of Sir Walter Mildmay, Chancellor of the Exchequer under Queen Elizabeth. In 1584 the queen noticed that Mildmay was absent from the court, and demanded an explanation. Put off by her suspicious, he replied, "Madam, I have been away planting an acorn, and when it becomes an oak, God only knoweth what it will amount to".

Mildmay had just founded Emmanuel College at Cambridge University, the Rev. John Harvard was one of the first graduates of Emmanuel. When Harvard was just twenty-eight, he immigrated to America and two years later he died leaving his library and half of his small estate to help endow a small college that today bears his name.

"From Emmanuel College, "Dr. Charles F. Thwing, writes, "came the founders of Harvard, the founders of New England, in a special sense, the founders of a new nation". It is no wonder that Mildmay didn't admit to good Queen Bess what he had done. He founded Emmanuel College on behalf of England's puritans, and the queen was definitely not a puritan. But those same puritans graduated from Emmanuel, emigrated to the America, and started colleges of their own among them are Harvard, Yale and Dartmouth, whose graduates include Samuel Adams, John Adams, Thomas Jefferson, and Daniel Webster, to name just a few of the founders and builders of this new America. That is the power of dreams.

4

'PARADIGM SHIFT'

PARADIGM SHIFT

The world is changing. People everywhere are sensing the difficulties our nations are facing. I feel the weight of it every time I see a newspaper or magazine with such captions "Hardship spread in the land", "Now the suffering continues", "Nigeria is in a mess". There are so many issues like political instability, people clamoring for the separation of this country, religious intolerance and extremism, the issue of resources control and derivation formula etc, but the one issue that is unsettling us most is our economic malaise. People can ignore or deny all other issues but cannot deny the state of their pocket, at least not far too long.

Massive structural changes are trying to shake our society. People have called these changes different names. "Future shock", "turning point", "paradigm shift", "massive changes". Whatever name is given, one thing for sure is that fundamental alterations in this nation's economy are taking place. All of this makes us feel unsettled.

Even under the best of circumstances, change is difficult. People don't like it. They tend to cling to old solutions. Tensions run high. Thomas Kuhn invented the popular buzz phrase "paradigm shift". In his book "the structure of scientific revolutions", he describes the reactions of scientists to new discoveries and how hard it has been for them to make changes in their basic beliefs. Kuhn noticed that scientists would go to any length to deny the validity of new theories or the need to change their minds. He describes the symptoms associated with fundamental change; persistent denial, refusal to consider evidence, reluctance to criticize old ideas, slander of new-thinking colleagues, and anger of having to give up cherished dogmas.

For sure we are not much different from those scientists. We feel uncomfortable with the changes in our lives; the social restructuring, the economic uncertainties. Our nation seems a little bit too unpredictable and we don't like it. We definitely don't like the government to control all economic businesses, but now we worry about what will replace it. We feel that free enterprise has shown great results, but we harbour concerns about its complete embracement.

With this book, other upcoming audio, video series and various seminars and workshops, I am launching "success way Inc," & Joseph Ager Foundation. Myself and a company of enthusiastic individuals who are underwriting this new corporation with me have these unclustered goals. We want to help build your faith in free enterprise, to shape your hope that it is possible to cope with the change and uncertainty we are facing, and to point to love as our guiding light for every step on the way forward.

We are also establishing/underwriting an "African centre for entrepreneurship development," a "Pan-African group for high-growth companies and a success unlimited venture—capitalist academy." From the beginning of 2005, we will be carrying our message of hope across the country and around the continent. We are determined to give a great deal of our lives, time, money and energy to helping people understand this free enterprise system and by so doing, helping our nation at large.

FREEDOM TO BE YOU

All over the world, men, women and children are stepping stunned and blinking into freedom's bright new day. It won't be easy to jump-start most of African's ruined economies. It is not going of course to be easy for us to turn our own economy around. But as long as we are free, the problem can be solved. We must resist anyone or anything that threatens our freedom no matter what "solutions" they offer us. Let those long years of military tyranny and wars remind us that without freedom all is lost.

We can dream great for ourselves and for others. Before Nelson Mandela could liberate his people he first had a dream Black South Africans at that time were denied the basic human rights that most of us in this country take for granted. They could not vote, speak out, write, or assemble freely. The law prohibited them from the benefits of free enterprise, of property ownership or even credit. It was some how even illegal for them to go to certain schools, let alone to own a home or business.

The forebears of today's black South Africans had little incentives to foster self-confidence or independence, let alone any inclination to become capitalists. The apartheid masters and bosses kept these Africans dependent and in debt. The majority of black South Africans lived in bondage to their employers and in fear of the lynch cobs.

Those tangled roots left generations of our fellow Africans feeling hopeless and helpless. Though some went on dreaming, but they could not exercise their powers to realize their dreams. It's not surprising today that crime is so rampant in South Africa and that most of these crimes are committed by the blacks who were produced by this tragic legacy.

Every man, woman and child is created in God's image, and because of that each has worth, dignity, and unique potential; therefore, you can dream great dreams for yourself and for others. You are not here on earth, born as an African, in this country and at this era by chance. No man is here by chance, you are here because God is in view of you. You matter to creation. You are not an ordinary citizen struggling for survival, but you have a part to play in this great economic revolution. Don't worry thinking maybe I'm trying to tune you to my own Christian tradition. You can be a successful free enterpriser and care less about God. You can believe in evolution with or without God's power and presence, and still make a go of anything in the business world. In the business world as you know, you don't have to be a Christian to be a success. There are fundamental laws that anybody who follows them succeeds. And that is why we have free thinkers, who have challenged every existence of God, but the question is; why were you created, and what are your dreams? What hopes do you have for seeing those dreams come true?

From where I come from, my Christian dream is built on love. Love heals. With Jesus as my example, I learned to forgive the past and dream great dreams for the future. And I'm passing on my free-enterprise dream to as many people that care to listen, to own their own successful businesses, and attain financial security. I'm free to use my time, money and creativity to serve others in this great nation.

LIVING YOUR POTENTIALS

"IF A MAN WANTS HIS DREAM TO COME TRUE HE MUST FIRST WAKE UP!"

I believe that most people feel that they are not living up to their potential and are grateful for any practical, realistic help they can get to change for the better. At some points in all of our lives, we all have a time when we feel our dreams are being frustrated and we will end up as failures. One thing for sure, whenever our dreams hit the rock we get the more frustrated, it's always been that way right from the start of time. Most of us live our lives in quiet desperation. In this nation for one, many shattered dreams have caused many sadness and unhappiness. But if we could get our lives together in times of despair, our body, soul and spirit might just as well be healthy.

Just be strong and know that God does exist. In out times of suffering, God is preparing us to help others who we will meet along the way. When our own dreams die, God is strengthening us to be there for our brothers and sisters when they lose dreams of their own. These are tough times for sure. Our dreams are threatened by forces beyond our control. Sometimes we lose the battle. But together we will win the war. With each other's help, we learn to dream again and then, one day, when we least expect it, we are surprised to see those dreams come true!

Most of us want the same opportunity of the rich and famous for ourselves and family. We dream of owning our own business. Dreaming of owning our own business is common among most young people of today. For some those dreams were already met and passed on to them from their parents and for others still, strong words of encouragement was passed on to them like "my son one day I know you'll be rich and own your business", "one day I know you will make us proud". Did you receive words like that? But for many, many others, they never hear such hopeful words from parents, teachers or friends. And so they rarely dream that they too can become great and be a star.

Generally though, we all dream to marry, raise good kids, own our home, have a large farm land, have a car and a reasonable source of income to be able to maintain a decent lifestyle and spend in the raining days ahead. Oh yes! We need these things; we all have in a way asked God for these things. So whether you want to be the one to come up with the cure of AIDS or the first woman president, you don't need to kill or cheat anyone to make your future.

Remember it is only the starting point to say, I want to be this or that with my life. Success is not a destination but a journey and in this journey of success, the first step always begins when you first try and in most cases our first steps ends in failures. It is the spirit of free enterprise that keeps us moving and makes the journey possible.

Free enterprise as I have always said is not great because it makes millions of dollars for a handful of people. It's because it helps millions of people to be what they want to be. For some whose dreams have been derailed, how do we get them back on the right track again

"CHANGE YOUR THOUGHTS AND YOU WILL CHANGE YOUR WORLD"

Most of the change we think we see in life is due to truths in favour or out of favour. Right now love is out of favour. If our institutions have failed or are failing, it is because they have forgotten that love comes first.

If the government is not doing its job, it's because those who govern have forgotten that every budget and money spent and every law should be based on love. If you want your productivity to increase, give love a chance in the market place. The great renewal we need as a people and as a nation will begin when individuals in these nations' great institutions begin again to love one another.

We live in a time when important institutions must be renewed and recreated. This is an age of opportunity, when we can forge new solutions, institutions and approaches to the problems that confront us. In the past, great crises have created great opportunities and civilizations have surged forward with new vitality.

If we work hard to discover and practice love again in our homes, schools, churches, businesses and in government, our economy would be turned around and our people could be set free to make life-changing dreams and with the help of each other we can reach them.

OPTIMISM

I know that free enterprise can lead to financial success for an individual, the community and the nation. Whatever talent you may possess can only spring up and be beneficial to you and your community when you are free to be you. Whatever you may need to succeed in business is useless without freedom. This book is a giant step towards that direction. I have no doubt that if everybody in a society are put on a fair playing field, millions of people will be inspired to be what they dreamed to become.

I call on you fathers of our land, I call on you mothers. I call on you young men, I call on you sisters to all become the thinkers of this generation. If this our generation fails to deliver Africa, she is doom for life. If the order of the day has been war and poverty and people being too deep in stiff-necked rivalry to control power and wealth, then I think turning to free enterprise presents the answers to a better and bright future for her. That is why I guess my approach as been carefully analyzed, to be highly interesting, logical and persuasive.

I have not only come to the defense of free enterprise which has made America so wealthy, but also I've set forth sure principles by which we can meet the morale and financial challenge of the twenty-first century. Anyone who takes his/her time to understand the guiding concepts of free enterprise will afterwards be better informed and more optimistic about the future of this great country.

This concept sets out a goal for us all to achieve and a way of helping ourselves by helping other people. While so many books have been written to define the American dream; and how to share in it, it is time now we begin defining the African dream' by giving an entirely appropriate name to the business philosophy which has been demonstrated by all wealthy countries in today's world. I'm trying to make us all richer by bringing to our fingertips the secret to the American dream and how this same secret can work for Africa.

It will work to restore the economic fortunes of Africa and cause an industrial, economic and information revolution for us all in one sweep. Having studied the lives of many successful individuals both within and outside the shores of this country, I can categorically state that they all possess one common denominator. And that is, they are all practitioners of free enterprise. Free enterprise is a mark of our commitment to generations yet unborn. If we refuse to accept this truth and embrace it, destiny will not forgive us. In a country that is actively practicing the mixed economy system this book is a must read for every aspiring entrepreneur ask those who have realized the personal successes of the other half-part of the economy that is in the free market system how prescriptive this free enterprise would heal our land.

If we can but embrace this free enterprise, we are truly free indeed to make our dreams come true by living our God given purpose, by showing the love of

God and of our country and by an authentic desire to help other people. It is my biggest hope that any one who grasp these facts will have his or her outlook on time, energy and money—which are the three most vital personal resource an individual possesses in our world—permanently changed. This free enterprise concept is not just for the would be successful entrepreneur' or that man/woman who has dreamed so longed to own his or her own business, but it is also for that sports man or woman, artist, writer, worker or employee. Because it is crystal clear, we all are in business and free enterprise is the key that will open the door to our success. I am glad at least to share this wisdom with you, all my dear friends.

AS YOU LIKE IT

It's been well over 40 years now since Nigeria got her independence. During most of this time, government has been in complete control and most directly influential to individual's life and quest to achieve their dreams of being in business for themselves. Beyond that and even more disturbing is the activities of some government tees to share only to themselves and their closest allies everything that comes out of the economy of this country. I have been inspired to develop and pass-on this same genuine concern of government controlling everything about business in our country to you.

Business or pleasures is filled with stories and examples of ordinary people both within and outside the shores of this country who simply refused to settle for mediocrity. The stories of these men reveal that you too can be a success in a free enterprise system as you will be given an equal chance to compete no matter your starting point and style. No doubt if we fully embrace the ideals of this system by privatizing and turning back all of the business enterprise in governments hands back to private ownership, initially it might be hard on the public but don't be afraid, we are overcomes. We all possess such a vast amount of abilities and God-given talents that we can't afford to take them to the grave still intact. For why! Business is all about people who have learned to believe in themselves and in a God that does not fail.

My desire is that after reading 'Business or Pleasures,' you too will experience the same feelings of hope, confidence, and optimism that I have. We too often live in a world where gloom and doom are always in the headlines. I encourage us to see the beautiful and remarkable world that we can create for ourselves. If only we will. I genuinely believe that all who read and grasp the concept of Free-enterprise, it will implant in their hearts the aspiration to pass on to future generations the opportunity to experience it.

MONEY

"THEY SAY MONEY ISN'T EVERYTHING. IT ISN'T EVERY-THING, BUT (IT) IS A GREAT BIG SOMETHING WHEN YOU ARE TRYING TO GET STARTED IN THE WORLD AND HAVEN'T ANYTHING. I SPEAK FEELINGLY"

—Thomas Watson

Money is only one symbol of wealth, and yet it is a very, very important form because it is symbolic of the true riches found in everything in the world. Most of us wonder if we ever will be able to pay all our bills in a month. Are you one of us? You have a dream, but you wonder if you will ever be able to afford that dream. You are employed all right, but before thirty days your pay-check is stretched to or even beyond the extreme. You may not be employed, but that does not exempt you from paying bills like rent, because you need to sleep under a roof, you need food on your table, you need to wear clothes! With all these needs pressing you hard day after day, you conclude with these words "if I'm going to see my dreams come true, I need to make more money". There just isn't anyway out for most of us. Money seems to be the answer to most of our problems.

"IT IS A KIND OF SPIRITUAL SNOBBERY THAT MAKES PEOPLE THINK THAT THEY CAN BE HAPPY WITHOUT MONEY"

—Albert Camus

"NO MAN WOULD HAVE REMEMBERED THE GOOD SAMARI-TAN IF HE'D ONLY HAD GOOD INTENTIONS. HE HAD MONEY AS WELL"

—Margaret Thatcher

Whether you agree with Saint Paul that "the love of money is the root of all evils", or you like rich dad's opinion, that, "the lack of money is the root of all evil", you will probably not argue that all of our waking up days and sleeping nights have thoughts of money and that getting and spending it worries us to some degree.

The good news is there are plenty of ways to make more money legally. But very disturbing is the news that so many still lunch themselves into illegal ways of making money. Godliness and contentment is great gain. Most people cause their money problem. They spend more than they earn.

IS MONEY EVIL?

"FOR THE LOVE OF MONEY IS THE ROOT OF ALL EVIL: WHICH WHILE SOME COVETED AFTER, THEY HAVE ERRED FROM THE FAITH, AND PIERCED THEMSELVES THROUGH WITH MANY SORROWS"

—I Timothy 6:10

Money is neither evil nor good. It is what you do with it that colours it with moral relativity. The same five hundred-naira note can feed a habit of smoking Indian hemp or put food on the table, pay for a prostitute, or buy your wife a bottle of perfume. Money simply makes you more of what you already were before you had it. If you were a giver before you had money, you will still be generous once you have wealth. If your focus was always the acquisition of riches, money will just feed your desires for more. Money shows your values and preferences. If I want to know who you really are, all I need to do is look at your spending habits. What you do with your money shows me what you love and value.

"MONEY IN THE HANDS OF AN UNBELIEVER IS OFTEN A SNARE, BUT IN THE HAND OF A CHILD OF GOD, IT CAN BE AN EFFECTIVE TOOL TO CARRY OUT THE GREAT COMMISSION"

—Mike Murdock

But the most important thing to take from Apostle Paul's words is that it is not money that is the root of all evil; it is the love of money that is evil. Don't let your money be your master. Finance is fickle, you could be riding high one day, and the next thing, and the winds of fortune will blow you off your mountain of money into a pit of poverty. Money cannot give you life. Money cannot give you love. Money cannot give you strength. Don't look to money for what only God can give you.

The "love of money" passage does not apply just to those who have, but also to those without. You can be dirt poor and have a greater heart of greed than a multimillionaire. Also, you can be so focused on your perceived godly state of poverty that, in a way, the love of money as the root of all evil applies to the pride you take in your state of lack.

AVOID BOTH EXTREMES

Neither extreme historic view of wealth is reflective of the scriptures or the heart of God for his people. The Apostle Paul eloquently put the role of wealth in it's proper place when he wrote, "not that I speak in respect of want: for I have learned, in whatever state I am, there with to be content. I know both how to be abased, and I know how to abound everywhere and in all things I am instructed both to be full and to be hungry, both to abound and to suffer need. I can do all things through Christ which strengthen me". (Philippians 4:11-13). He says he was contented in both states. That doesn't mean that he lacked ambition, for he was not controlled by his drives. He was motivated by his purpose Paul knew how to do all things through Christ whether he had stuff or not, whether he had food on the table or not. Regardless of his financial state, he learned to draw contentment from Christ. Paul idolizes neither lack nor abundance; he simply puts them in their proper perspective. The focus is not on the amount in the account, but on the amount of contentment and strength drawn from the Christ in the heart.

Our brother the monk and our brother the prosperity preacher have failed to understand the essence of Christianity. The Christian experience is one that transcends the issues of abundance or lack, and provides a contentment and peace that carries the believer through the ricissitudes of life's bull and bear markets, full and empty pantries, and abounding or overdrawn bank accounts. "I can do all thing through Christ," means that he is my focus of existence. He is my source of contentment and the one who, through wants and release my prosperity in the increments I can handle. It is not because I am such a good sheep. It is that, he is the good Shepherd that I shall not want! Pray this prayer with me: if you don't mind—

<Lord, heal me from the stress and the pressure that I get from worrying about my perception among my peers. Give me the gift of being satisfied by what you want me to have and when you know I can handle it. I thank you that you are teaching me to walk beside you and not in front of you. I repent for the times I got ahead of you. I regret the times you were trying to bless me and I was somewhere behind you, groveling with old issues. From this day forward I walk with you in peace and prosperity, knowing who I am, where I am, and whose I am. I am prepared to be blessed financially with the practical steps I am learning. But my focus is on you, for now I know that you are the greatest richness attainable and when I seek you first other things will happen as I prepare myself for what you have for me. Thank you for maturity coming to me spiritually, financially, and emotionally. My family will be blessed by what you are teaching me now. Amen>

WORK

"IF ANYONE DOES NOT WORK, HE SHOULD NOT EAT"

People are being sacked everyday, and go home to face their families with such depressing news. Unemployment in Nigeria has gulp almost sixty-six percent of the work force and more than seventy percent of this nation's population live below the poverty line.

With more and more Nigerians adding to the long queue of unemployment every passing year than the previous, it may seem a strange time to suggest and stick to the phrase "anyone that does not work should not eat. Most people will reply "I want to work but no work to do". Of course when you are unemployed, you're glad for any work at all. "A beggar" they say "has no choice". Still some are employed but are very unhappy with their work and worth. And as you know, those with the lowest level of satisfaction in their work and worth are mainly unionized workers, clerical workers, younger workers and all those with lower incomes.

Since the beginning of time, work has been for many people a terrible, inescapable fact of life. Rich explains it like this. The ancient Greeks thought that the necessity to work was proof that the gods hated them. The Romans felt the same way. The word for work, in both of those civilizations, comes from a root, which meant "sorrow". The Romans felt that work demeaned intelligent people. They thought that only the contemplative life (thinking, not working) deserved respect.

In the middle ages, work was dirty and difficult. Peasants spent their life-times shoveling dirt, getting it on their shoes and underneath their fingernails, smelling it on their skin and picking it out of their hair. And ordinary people didn't even get paid for all that shoveling. They worked because they had to. Life was work and work was life. They could not leave the jobs they had inherited from birth and go somewhere else. They usually were born, worked, and died on the same tract of land-land that they could shovel but could not own.

About the time of the Renaissance, ideas about work began to change. People like the Roman Catholic Scholar Thomas Aquinas began to think that work wasn't so bad after all. Maybe God didn't hate workers. Work was a duty and a burden, to be sure, but perhaps it was a natural right as well. Gradually people's long-held negative feelings about work began to shift.

During and after the Reformation, attitudes changed more quickly. Martin Luther boldly proposed that work, instead of being a curse from God, was really a way of serving God—an act similar to worship. Luther helped give work dignity. He made it more than meaningless drudgery.

John Calvin, the Geneva reformer, advanced the revolution in thinking about work. In fact, he influenced ideas about work so much that he has been credited with planting the first seeds of free enterprise. For Calvin, work was like ministry. Work was good. He thought that people ought to work and use their abilities to the fullest.

That work could be good was a new idea in the days of Luther and Calvin. (It is a new idea for many of us still). And if it was hard to believe that work was good, imagine people surprise when they were told that they had a God-given right to do meaningful work, work they enjoyed, work that led to self—esteem.

People used to think that you could work only at those occupations your family or social class were supposed to do. Calvin liberated the idea of work from this bondage and encouraged people to take the greatest possible initiative, to explore their own gifts and talents and to put them to work.

Many of the ideas we have about work, including the freedom to choose any career we want, are fairly new. I am convinced that work—meaningful work—provides benefits to people that go far beyond just earning money to trade for food and shelter. And I thank Aquinas, Luther, Calvin and the others who made it possible for us to think that meaningful work would enhance and ennoble our lives.

When work is pleasure; life is joy! When work is a duty life is slavery. Successful people gain a sense of mastering themselves—overcoming their fears and doubts—and of mastering their environment—gaining a sense of independence and freedom from want via meaningful work. So work is a powerful force in shaping a person's sense of identity.

Meaningful work also gives people the knowledge that they are making a difference in the world, increasing the wealth and welfare of their nation, and achieving a better standard of living for themselves and their children.

Entrepreneurs say that their enjoyment of meaningful work often springs from a deep interest in some hobby or other pursuit. We are spurred to action when we notice that something is missing in the world, and we begin to think about undertaking a project or business to fill that gap. Modern entrepreneurs often find meaningful work to be play. They take action in order to discover, or to serve, and in the process transform or improve the world.

Nigerian entrepreneurs will particularly become motivated to do meaningful work by the spirit of free enterprise, by the freedom of choice, we will enjoy and have the opportunity to go as far as our ambition and hard work can carry us. It is usually at the worst financial times that many people discover their own entrepreneurial spirit, and what a difference this could make.

I RECALL THE STORY OF THE FARMER WHO, WHEN ASKED BY HIS NEIGHBOR WHY HE WAS WORKING HIS SONS SO

HARD JUST TO GROW CORN, HE REPLIED, 'I'M NOT JUST GROWING CORN, I'M GROWING SONS".

—Kenneth Blanchard.

The free enterprise system is inclusive and should embrace all people. We all have the right to work regardless of our race, nationality, skin colour, regional or tribal background, religious beliefs age, physical illness or disability, gender, or sexual orientation. Wherever freedom is denied to anyone for unfair or unjust reasons, free enterprise cannot thrive. The freedom to become an entrepreneur or choose our occupation is a freedom of immeasurable value.

You can go to the depths of despair and still come out on top. Women might have to work harder to get to the top, but Carolyn Stradley who is a beautiful example of this statement says it's worth it". As a young mother of twenty-six, her husband died, and all her efforts to get the capital to start her own business was refused by several banks for so many years. She didn't quit, she didn't sell her body. She worked harder and eventually got the money from a credit company to start her own construction business. Yes, she is in the construction business, but her mind is not like concrete-it is not all mixed up and permanently set! She expects to make over a hundred thousand dollars this year. She travels to other countries, scuba dives, sky dives, camps with her daughter, and still works twelve hours a day. She knows that even though she has an idea, a dream, the most practical, beautiful, workable philosophy in the world won't work—if she doesn't work.

I want men to understand this fact; not every woman is living on wishes for the privilege of finding a man someday to take her home. Some of the most attractive women are ladies with a mind and a will of their own. Their lives are consumed by ferocious self-discipline, isolation, and work. They neither smoke nor drink, they don't sell their bodies to make a living but are constantly finding ways to advance their lives and positions. If you find such, help her. Why do such women push so hard? Most times, it's not for the money anymore, but for the love of helping others, and a feeling of responsibility to other women.

Women, set your goals. Work with intense desire, and you will make it. It is definitely worth the hardship and the discipline. You too can become a successful entrepreneur, and too you can appreciate the fact that you don't "pay the price" to succeed, you enjoy the price of success. Remind yourself that anything worth having is worth working for—and then go to work.

Often the difference between success and failure is simply desire. The footballer with his team, the salesman with his product, the mother with her children, or the student with his studies—all must have a deep desire to excel. Of all the factors that help lead to success [and there are many!] perhaps nothing is more important than simple raw desire and determination to succeed. The football player running with the ball has one-goal determination to get the ball behind the goal line. The mother who spends twenty-four hours each day with her little one must have lots of love and a tremendous desire to give her children the best possible preparation for life.

The salesman who goes out each day to sell his product is also one who must have desire. He must know the right sales techniques, know his product and believe in it, have some knowledge of prospective customer, and know how to give his sales presentation. But unless the salesman truly has the desire to sell, he will not be successful. The salesman can know all the techniques involved, the footballer can be a fantastic football player, the mother can have all the answers, the student can be very brainy but without an overwhelming desire to succeed each one will not climb as high as his or her ability actually allows. What about you? Are you pursuing that deep—down desire of your life? Are you striving toward the goal of your choice? If you will, then eliminate distractions and place your task in order of importance or priority, and work, work, work!

Isn't it amazing to know what adapting a simple system can do to our entrepreneurial spirit? Let me make it clear that I'm not trying to persuade anyone of going into business. But people should go where their entrepreneurial spirit leads them. What kind of rewards would follow if you gave time, energy and hard work to your dreams?

"I WANT TO BE THOROUGHLY USED UP WHEN I DIE, FOR THE HARDER I WORK, THE MORE I LIVE".

—George Bernard Shaw.

TIME

"WASTE YOUR MONEY AND YOU'RE ONLY OUT OF MONEY, BUT WASTE YOUR TIME AND YOU'VE LOST A PART OF YOUR LIFE".

—Michael LeBoeuf

The most important resource that is available to man is time. Every second counts. Every second is valuable. And every second lost can never be recovered, it only passes by once. Life is short, remember and no man will spend eternity here on earth. The Bible says, "Redeeming the time, because the days are evil". [Ephesians 4:28 & 5:16]. So we must make the best opportunity of every second and get as much as we possible can, done in the shortest time frame.

The earlier you make your money the more valuable it will serve you. The sooner you start investing the earlier you get the returns. Fifty Naira today will be less valuable in some couple of years later. But if Fifty Naira is invested today it will yield much more in a couple of years and not withstanding the depreciation on the value of money, your money is also multiplying. And you could have even more to spend on the things you want. So the sooner you begin an investment or savings program the better for you. Don't stockpile money for it to depreciate, instead invest it for it to appreciate. Don't wait for a boom to start your savings. Start it from now with the little you have in your hands.

The saying goes, "Time is Money." Thank God, time is a factor of equality, that is, there is equal time for every thing on earth. It's twenty-four hours for every one in a day. This makes the millionaire and the pauper alike in at least one respect-each one is given 1,440 minutes of time everyday. Yet most people constantly complain that they don't have enough time.

Proper time management is a must for every successful person. Time is our most important commodity. When those moments and hours slip away they do not return; they are gone forever. The question is how do you effectively use your time? In attempting to answer the question of time management, one must begin to realize that there aren't sixty minutes in every hour as it looks.

As a practical matter, there are only as many minutes in the hour as you can use. How many hours are you wasting?

If you really want to know you will take a serious inventory. Use a calendar or appointment book and mark it off in eight-hour slots. Now mark off the hours into sixty-minutes segments. As you go through each day this week track of where your time is going by writing down what you do during those sixty-minutes time frames. Do it for one week. Then go back and check your book. You'll be surprised when you realize that hours and hours of time are wasted on nonessential items due to procrastination and poor organization.

Remember that time really is the only thing you have to sell to yourself or anyone else. The better use you make of your time, the higher the price you will be paid for it. And on the other hand also, the longer you have to wait for money the less the value of the money. Don't forget, it even cost money to wait. You must spend money every passing day even if you're waiting. So think right-now of any profitable cycle that will also bring that money back to you because water runs dry.

"HE WHO MASTERS HIS TIME, MASTERS HIS LIFE"

—Mike Murdock

5

'THE FOUR INDISPENSIBLE PRINCIPLES TO BUSINESS SUCCESS'

THE FOUR INDISPENSIBLE PRINCIPLES TO BUSINESS SUCCESS

The top is your heritage. Success is your birthright but there are certain principles, you need to follow to get there.

Just working hard is not the key to success. There are people who have great strength and power they work hard and consistently but still don't succeed. Working hard is not the key to success; people could work hard but still be a failure. You may work as hard as you want and never see success and wealth, so there must be something in addition to hard work. There is another important key that is needed to add to hard work.

"IF THE AXE IS DULL AND IT'S EDGE IS UNSHARPENED, THEN MUCH STRENGTH IS NEEDED BUT WITH SKILL, SUCCESS COMES"

—Ecclesiastes 10:10

An axe is an instrument to achieve something with; if it's not sharp you won't get much result. Solomon is stressing a principle here. He says that having an axe, meaning having a dream, a vision, a gift, a talent, a good business idea is not just enough. If the axe is dull and unsharpened, you will work hard and get little done. When you sharpen an axe you work less and achieve more. So when you have a sharpened axe, you will work with precision, not just hard. In the next statement he says, "but with skill, success comes". So, it is skill that makes a business successful. You need skill. Skill is not prayed for, skill is not a gift, skill is obtained through training—getting all the relevant information you need to make your business successful.

Now before we go further, let quickly look at the four different levels of wealth that exist in our society today.

Level 1:   When you are being employed—At this level, where you're being employed by another, someone else controls your destiny.

Level 2:   When you have your own business—At this level, you have your own business; however, it's not the best way. It's not a too good level because you're bearing all the risk alone.

Level 3:   When people work for you—At this stage, you just oversee while people are working for you. It's, but, a much better level.

Level 4:   When you gain money while you're sleeping—This of course is the highest and the greatest level. When you make money while you sleep. The wealthiest people in the world are people who just make money while they sleep. To get to this 4th level however, you must pass through and experience all the first three level. It's not automatic or overnight to get to this 4th level.

However, this shouldn't be surprising. You earn money while you sleep, in things like investment, shares, stocks, royalties and bonds. At that level, you are not suppose to work for money but money work for you. At this junction, I would like to say this truth straight; the kingdom of God needs as many wealthy people that it can get.

So now we can look at the four secret keys for business success as advocated by Myles Munroe. I believe as we take a dive into them, we will be bold enough to venture into any adventure concerning quality business ideas since now; we will be trading with facts.

This principles are God's principles according to Dr. Myles Munroe, and everything you need to know about life is contained in the book of Genesis, chapter one and two of the Bible. These are the only two perfect chapters in the Bible where God himself declared, "this is good" all through. Every successful business enterprise has used God's principles to succeed. God, in Genesis chapter one verse twenty-eight enacted four principles of business success:

NO1 PRINCIPLE

BE FRUITFUL: God said "be fruitful" not "be seedful". Whatever God calls for, he provides for. Everyman posses seed. God demands fruits because he has put a seed inside you. That business idea, that concept, that dream, and even that product is a seed. In Hebrew, the word 'fruitful' means 'productive' produce something unique out of it. Everybody is carrying a seed that has a produce the world needs. The seed of greatness is in everybody. A product of unique seasoning that nobody else has, like Kentucky Chickens, McDonalds, etc. produce something that is unique and that is yours.

God's word is emphatic "be fruitful", in other words, the word of God is saying have "a product", not "products". Every tree produces only one kind of fruit not different kinds of fruits. If you want to be successful in business, pick that one thing you dream and think about it, develop it, refine it, define and exploit it. Learn about it, and develop a fruit that is yours out of it. Don't be a jack-of-all-trades! Nothing can make you poor faster than being a jack of all trade. Don't try to do everything! Don't sell everything!

God is saying every tree always produce one kind of fruit. Jesus our greatest came to do one thing—to die on the cross. So all you need to do is produce something that's you—develop your own product, your product is what people think about when they hear your name. At this point, I think some fellows may need to seclude themselves, spend time alone in a very quiet place (any you can think of; like maybe a mountain) and ask God "what I'm going to be good at? Zero in, on it, and give you life a focus. That will take you away from the camp of the confused and make you a first class citizen.

NO 2 PRINCIPLE

MULTIPLY: if you are going to be successful in business, you've got to develop a product that can be multiplied. "Multiply" in this context means to "duplicate". You can never be successful in business if you cannot duplicate what you produce. The first thing Jesus did was to be fruitful, the He kept multiplying till today. There were only twelve people in Jesus' university, but since after His departure the world has not recovered from its effect. McDonalds once had one hamburger, but they kept multiplying it and duplicating it over and over again. Produce a product you can multiply if not, you'll keep sowing for everybody and that's not good business. My books are a fruit that are now multiplied, duplicated all over the place! Nigeria for instance has amazing products but we don't believe in our products, so we can't even multiply them. ""Don't be limited by circumstances and mediocrity don't settle for less than God's best for you, God's best is for you to saturate the world with what you produce. This brings us to the third principle.

NO 3 PRINCIPLE.

REPLENISH: The word "replenish" means distribute". Don't just produce and multiply it, distribute it far and wide until the whole earth is filled with your "fruit"—your "product", your "skill". God is always wise. You can't produce, then multiply and keep. You must distribute. And this is the most major factor that people often miss-out. The most successful companies in the 21st century will be the companies that cannot only produce and multiply fruit, distribution is going to be the key. This explains why the Internet is a blessing from God. Don't produce what you can't distribute! Successful businesses are able to sell their products to the market. Now to successfully distribute, sometimes you may require merging. You need to engage in 'networking' that is merging with other people in the same field of business in order to distribute your product.

So if you must be successful in business you will have to contact networking. Remember, Jesus did merge with John the Baptist. Joseph who had the key to save his country still needed to be in pharaoh's castle so as to contact networking. Nehemiah worked with the king that was networking. Daniel did the same. All of these are biblical examples. Jesus himself did advice us to make friends with the world. Dr. Myles Munroe has to work with circular bookstores to get his books all over America. Its only then, an unbeliever who could easily walk to a circular bookstore could pick up one of his books and became saved. "Distribution"!

NO 4 PRINCIPLE

SUBDUE: The word "Subdue" means to "dominate" or "control" the market, dominate the market of the people. Every successful business in the world dominates the market. Learn how to distribute and then dominate. Japan's products; Sony, Mitsubishi, Toshiba, Toyota etc are all over Nigeria for instance, why? Because they the Japanese have learnt distribution and domination.

Bill Gates is the wealthiest man in the world today because he followed God's direction in these principles. He has observed God's principle more than we do. He is so successful in producing, duplicating, distributing and dominating the market—the entire world with his fruit. If you are determined to become a Bill Gate, you too can become very successful when you apply these four principles. I say to you prophetically, be fruitful, multiply, replenish the earth, subdue the market and have dominion in Jesus name! Amen.

THE PURPOSE THING

Here we are friends; every successful business used God's principles to succeed. In the book of Luke chapter sixteen, where we saw Jesus teaching at greatest management seminar, He said, "go to the world and learn from them". Why? Because they are wise in their own dealings. Wisdom therefore entails the effective application and use of the principles just shared.

The first question, however, is "why did God create me"? Now, in Genesis chapter two from verse four beginning, the bible clarified that God allowed no development, progress, no advancement, He held up the rain and made sure nothing was happening, why? Because there was no man to manage it. Nevertheless, God brought those things when He created man. That is to say, you and I were created to be a manager', God's motivation for creating man was managing. So God can only trust you with what you can manage. It doesn't matter what you pray for and for how long you've prayed for it, God will only give you what you can manager. Don't forget quickly the line from Jesus management seminar in Luke sixteen, "if you can be trusted with little, I will trust you with more" if you can't manage other peoples job, God is not going to give you yours.

You need to be able to manage everything under your control including your time, what you need and even what you eat and drink. Of course; it's always easier to be employed than to be deployed. Whatever you mismanage, you loose. To be an effective businessperson you must cultivate proper management ability. Be accountable for every cent and everything.

Please, note this very carefully: in Genesis chapter one verse twenty-six where God made known His management intention, in all the items we where created to dominate, man was not found in the list. So we were not created to dominate people. No human was created to be dominated (and that's also including the female gender factor). Let's look at it very clearly now:

"SO GOD CREATED MAN IN HIS OWN IMAGE, IN THE IMAGE OF GOD HE CREATED HIM; MALE AND FEMALE HE CREATED THEM. GOD BLESSED THEM AND SAID TO THEM, "BE FRUITFUL AND MULTIPLY, AND REPLENISH THE EARTH ANDSUBDUE IT. RULE OVER THE FISH OF THE SEA AND THE BIRDS OF THE AIR AND OVER EVERY LIVING CREATURES THAT MOVES ON THEGROUND"

—Genesis 1:26

See that! To bless in this instance means to demand and call for hidden potentials. God's original purpose for man is dominion. We have already seen how we are suppose to do it—remember, dominion has nothing to do with domineering people, but it is with environment and resources—never you forget the four instructional manual.

Then you will have dominion

6

'WAKE UP
AND GET UP'

WAKE UP AND GET UP

"Far better it is to dare mighty things, to win glorious triumphs, even though checkered by failure, than to take rank with those poor spirits who neither enjoy much nor suffer much, because they live in the gray twilight that knows neither victory nor defeat".

—Theodore Roosevelt

There is a gold mine hidden in every life. God never made a failure. Everyman has success hidden deep inside of him. No one else can find it but himself. He holds the key to the hidden room. Failure comes because we never sough that hidden treasure. Failure comes because we tried to find it somewhere else. You can't find it anywhere else. Success, victory, achievement are all in you. There is a millionaire in you. The exceptional people are those who develop what is within them.

The few who are winning fame and success are doing so because they developed what they had in them. Single handedly, maybe you can't do it but with teamwork, you definitely will do it. The top musicians, sport stars, great preachers all had it in them and they developed it and made it of commercial value.

Many folks have misplaced their destiny because of laziness. They prefer the companion of drinking men and worthless women if not they would have been known the world over. Some have even be able to identify their abilities but never amounted to anything. They did not develop the thing that was in them. Genius has grown up with weeds about it, just because they did not develop the thing they had. I know it is hard work but you will learn to love hard work. There are no great gold nuggets lying on top of the earth now. You have to go down into the earth for them; you must dig for them.

"MONEY FLOWS IN THE DIRECTION OF LABOUR"

You want the applause of the world? You want money to buy fine clothes and build splendid houses? Awaken young men. Go fine that hidden place in your own nature. Dig and dig until you have conquered.

The story was told about a father who was dying. He had two sons. The boys had always felt that he had gold that he had hidden away somewhere. He had never been a strong, healthy man so his farm was not developed. Back of the house there was ten acres of stump land. When he was dying he said, "The stump lot". Again and again he said "The stump lot". As soon as the funeral was over the boys said. "The gold is out in the stump lot". How feverishly they worked. They tore up every inch of it. But they found no gold. Then the older one said "we have the land in good condition, let's put in corn". In the harvest, they found in the ripened corn the gold. You have a stump lot in you. Dig it up, clean it up, and you will find the gold in it.

Nothing will take the place of hard work, intelligently directed. The talents in you need push and determination to make them worth money. It is you and you alone who will do the developing. The lazy person who waits for something to turn up is a failure. The only things that will turn up are rents, bills and responsibilities. Nothing will take the place of self-denial and hard work.

It is easy to become a failure; all you need to do idly dream. It is the man who wills and keeps on willing who wins. Don't float. Don't wait for an opportunity. Go make your opportunity. Put your whole self into life. Pay the initial price, study hard, and drive yourself. Always remember that your worst enemy is inside of you.

No circumstance, no person or combination of persons can conquer you as long as you do not destroy your own prospects yourself. Don't be satisfied with anything you do. Always seek to improve yourself.

Take an inventory again and again and see what you possess; see whether that possession is more valuable today than it was a year ago. Find where your ability lies. Then put all of your best in that ability and make that ability come across and put you over. Remember that what you have hungered and yearned to do, you have the ability to do—if you will.

ALL HARDWORK BRINGS PROFIT, BUT MERE TALKS LEADS ONLY TO POVERTY"

—Proverbs 14:23

Bring Your Ideas to Reality.

Many individuals have difficulty bringing their ideas to reality. For some many people, their ideas though very creative, do not see the light of the day, because they lack the where withal to create a new venture.

Although those in this group continue to bemoan their fate, many businesses are being formed all over the world each day despite recession, inflation, lack of infrastructure etc. The creations of new ventures go through processes.

Identify Opportunities:

To be a good entrepreneur, the individual must be able to discover opportunities that are not seen or known by others. The perspective entrepreneur may arrive at this through acquiring the necessary information either through exposure to new ideas or reading wide.

However, mere discovery of opportunity does not create wealth, as much as possible; the discovery should culminate in investment.

Reduce Your Uncertainty:

Due to fear of the unknown, even when an individual has a good idea, putting it into practice is always postponed and procrastination we know could be very dangerous.

To reduce this rather high state of uncertainty, the individual should immediately determine the viability of the idea. This could be achieved through the use of available information and going out for more information on the subject matter.

Exercise Your Options:

Usually, more than one idea can crop up, but a particular option must be implemented, at least one at a time.

To do this successfully, the individual must be creative enough to identify follow-on opportunities that are necessary to maximize profit, especially if the option continues to appear lucrative.

Know When to Quit:

Closure process in entrepreneurship involves the termination of business that were launched but which are no longer viable. An entrepreneur that is on alert should be able to know when to discontinue investing in a business that is not yielding.

This has to do with the decision to terminate the business by the founders, when they realize that their business is no longer as lucrative as it should be. The point here is that the individual should not wait for the business to go under before thinking of closing shop.

"The average entrepreneur sees opportunities that others do not perceive or care about and uses relevant data and information to create something new" says Mrs. Solabomi Ajibolade. According to her, the great goal of our entrepreneurs from an economic perspective is wealth creation even though there may be several other motivating factors as financial attraction, desire for independence/security and fear of sudden disruption in a salary job.

Between you and your wealth, there may be many a swamp through which a road must be made. Just as lumberman always builds roads to the timber they wish to market. So also you will have to build a road to market your abilities. There is pain and fatigue ahead for you, but you dress for the job. Remember to associate with people who have won those who help you climb to the top.

Don't hang around with a group of "has been". Associate with men who are climbing up. The idle, gossiping people will not help you. The lazy and careless will stand in your way. Those who spend their nights in the brothel house or at the gambling hall will never help you. Don't think you can get something for nothing. Put your money where it will count. Put your time where it will pay you dividends. This battle is not for the thoughtless, heedless guesser or idealistic dreamer. It is for the man who works. You can do it!

"I LONG TO ACCOMPLISH A GREAT AND NOBLE TASK, BUT IT IS MY CHIEF DUTY TO ACCOMPLISH HUMBLE TASKS AS THOUGH THEY WERE GREAT AND NOBLE. THE WORLD IS MOVED ALONG, NOT ONLY BY THE MIGHTY SHOVES OF ITS

HEROES, BUT ALSO BY THE AGGREGATE OF THE TINY PUSHES OF EACH HONEST WORKER"

—Attributed to Helen Keller.

MENTAL CALCULUS

"IF THERE IS ANYTHING IN THE WORLD THAT CAN REALLY BE CALLED A MAN'S PROPERTY, IT IS SURELY THAT WHICH IS THE RESULT OF HIS MENTAL ACTIVITIES"

For many people, building that financial empire is a guarded secret revealed to some chosen few. Where the problem lies is that we look outward for what is actually inward. Just as they say happiness, joy or worry is a State of the mind, in the same vein. Wealth is the result of a very specific mental attitude.

"WEALTH IS A STATE OF THE MIND".

Money is the outward manifestation of an inner focus and thoughts steered towards a specific target. The mind is capable of anything. Genuine wealth is, above all a state of mind—a state that has taken form in the lives of the rich. We must begin by being rich in mind before we can become rich in life.

"WEALTH IS THE RESULT OF MANS CAPACITY TO THINK".

Until you put your mind to work nothing works. Therefore gaining a clear understanding of the subconscious is fundamental. People must believe in success and fortune, and want it passionately. You deserve to have money-lots of money—and you can easily be rich. Money no doubt is important, and more money is better than less money. The concepts presented in this chapter will help you think rich and get rich. They will give you deeper, more powerful insights into what money really is.

Love, Sex and money are words that command instant attention. They are so vital that to be completely successful requires that one has the right attitude about them. So, let's turn our attention to the joy of having enough money—not just enough to get by, but more than enough so we can enjoy complete financial independence!

PUTTING YOUR MIND TO WORK

The mind is the capital for any business exploit. It is the seat of your power. Business is thinking. If you are not a thinker, you can't have a place in the business world. As said earlier that wealth is the result of man's capacity to think. Engaging the mind for strategic thinking to come up with definite concrete plans and execution method is what makes for a successful enterprise. All the men and women of exploits in the business world are people that engaged strategic thinking to come up with strategic investment which gave birth to their universal dominance.

The capital you need for any meaningful business exploits is not money but your mind. Money is only a means to an end. This is why without the right mental calculus with all the money you will still go bankrupt. But with the right mental calculation and no money you will still build the biggest business empire ever known by man. So what you need to become a man and women of exploits is not bucks but brains. You can loose all the bucks you've inherited without proper brainwork. You can also make all the bucks you've ever imagined with just brainwork.

So, that thing you carry on your neck called head is not for decoration, but for exploits in every area of your life. Apart from those who are mentally retarded, due to complications in the formation of their brains, it's been discovered that all humans have the same number of brain cells. Also surprising to know is the fact that with all the inventions in the world, man has barely been able to use ten percent of the four billion brain cells. Can you pause and imagine what could happen if man tries to use fifteen percent of his brains? I think you'll be out of space. Unfortunately though, most of us are using barely one percent.

Where most people have problem understanding this thinking theory is when they take it to be education. With all due respect to education, I won't be sorry though to point out clearly that education is not common sense. Education, just like money should be viewed as a means to the end, but not the end itself. Education should never be mistaken or given the place of thinking, reasoning or mental calculation. No doubt though, education is the foundation and the most integral element of our learning process, and preparation for any meaningful life. It is the bedrock of meditation because you only think on the things you can read, hear, see and understand.

However, education is not wisdom, while education is the acquiring of relevant knowledge at ones disposal, wisdom on the other hand is the accurate application of the knowledge acquired. So, the dividing line is simple, education helps us to know how to read and reading opens the door to the bank of knowledge and information. If you can read, you could learn just about anything you want to know. The doors of the world are open to readers. Just as St. Paul told Timothy, "give attendance to reading". Because reading is the only way to improve your mind effectively. Nothing enhances and brightens your chances in life like reading. John Mason makes us to understand that, "your life won't be different in ten years time except for two things: the books you read and the people you associate yourself with". More than anything else, these two affects our lives.

The Richest man in the world, Bill Gates is a great thinker. He loved to think hard and calculate. Though Gates dropped out of school to face his computer business, he always kept his mind busy by always thinking of what could be done to get things done better and faster. The story was told about an instance when once the mother called him several times and he didn't answer. When she finally found him sitting at the basement of their staircase, she yields "didn't you hear me calling you" Gates replied, "Mum, I am thinking, or don't you think? As far as young Gates was concerned, if your brain would work and produce result, you should talk less.

"EVERY STAR IS A THINKER, AND EVERY THINKER IS A POTENTIAL STAR"

—Bishop David Oyedepo

PROSPERITY MINDEDNESS

Prosperity mindedness is a positive belief system—nothing more, nothing less. Your mind has two major functions. Conscious (objective) and subconscious (subjective). Although separate in their reaction to stimuli and data, they are not divided or in opposition to each other. At any given moment your mind can act upon only one primary belief.

When you send two ideas and feelings that are opposite in nature, your mind will only act upon the dominant one. When you study the life of the rich, it will reveal that each one of them made full use of their subconscious mind to become wealthy. The key of success ultimately lies in the proper use of the subconscious mind. Why? You might ask. The reason is that both the means to make money and the outside circumstances affecting us are so varied and personal that it would be impossible to propose a sure-fire winning formula. Besides, no miracle recipe exists. It would be too ordinary. What does exist, however, and thousands of brilliant success stories testify to this, is a positive inner attitude.

No matter how instructive a book claims to be, it will not tell you whether you should accept a job that comes your way, bid on a property or invest in a particular money making proposition. Each case is unique. Even if your preliminary studies are very comprehensive, there are always imponderables in any scheme. Any analysis will be inadequate. This is when a persons sixth sense, some people also call 'business sense', 'Luck', or 'intuition', comes into play—the result of positive mental programming and a well-utilized subconscious mind. This is what makes the difference between a successful and an unsuccessful person.

"WEALTH, VIEWED IN ITS PROPER SENSE, IS A MEANS OF INCREASING ONE'S OWN CREATIVITY, A PHASE IN THE EVOLUTION OF THE HUMAN RACE".

—Leonard Reed

HOW TO FIND WEALTH

"BUT THOU SHALT REMEMBER THE LORD THEY GOD: FOR IT IS HE THAT GIVETH THEE POWER TO GET WEALTH, THAT HE MAY ESTABLISH HIS COVENANT WHICH HE SWORE UNTO THY FATHERS, AS IT IS THIS DAY".

—Deuteronomy 8:18

I often times ask myself this question, "how can getting rich and staying rich be simpler"? it's been said again and again by government and leaders, over the years also we've read books upon books and listened tirelessly to sermons that promises to make us rich or at least better our lives. But most times, sorry to say, it ends up the same old way—failed promises. They say you should do this, and they say you can't do that. And we are tempted to ask, "What does life really want from us"? We know money doesn't grow on trees, but where exactly does it grow? In our heads? Well the truth of the matter is, the key to wealth can be summed-up in just one word. Simplicity. Keep this in mind, it's very simple.

Though there is always a wilderness experience in every man's journey in life, don't faint, don't fret. God is only weaning you just like He did to the children of Israel when He brought them out of Egypt after four hundred years f bondage. As a people, their hands of initiative were tied and feet of self-progress were shackled. God simply had to wean the children of Israel from the reliance on others. So, He led them out of Egypt into the wilderness. Surely, of course, one of the most damaging traits that subverts and impedes the progress of any people is dependency on others. To be reliant on someone else's kindness is an extremely vulnerable experience. To depend on someone else for your livelihood is to open yourself for serious wounds and bruises. So God wants us to stay strong, He wants us to be self-reliant, and greater still God reliance.

Prosperity begins with strength for the journey. It goes far beyond surviving to thriving. But it starts with strength for the day. God delivered the children of Israel from the wilderness to more than enough (Deuteronomy 8:7-9). This is where God wants us to be as well. He is the one that gives us the power to get wealth. However, your seed of greatness will not grow without you using your faith to stretch yourself beyond your past limitations. Truth is you need to work together with God, put into action the gifts He has given you, then you too will be brought to a place of abundance. God wants you to get wealth. He wants you to be financially independent. He wants you to use your faith to unlock your finances. Remember it is He that gives you the power to make wealth. Howbeit there is a little warning in that passage of the scripture; lets take another critical look at it.

"Beware that thou forget not the Lord thy God, in not keeping His commandments, and His judgments, and His statutes, which I command. Thee this day: lest when thou has eaten and art full, and has built goodly houses, and dwelt therein: And when thy herds and they flocks multiplied, then thine heart be lifted up, and thou forget the LORD they God, which brought thee forth out of the land of Egypt, from the house of bondage…"

—Deuteronomy 8:11-14

And just like the children of Israel, you can forget the Lord. When you get to your place of abundance, when you begin to enjoy prosperity, you must not say in your heart, "my power and the might of mine hands hath gotten me this wealth" (Deuteronomy 8:17). Most of us remember God when we are in crisis. We pray because we are in some kind of trouble, but the moment the trouble subsides, we forget our prayers. We no longer count our blessings, because we have become too busy counting our money. We become completely blind by our good fortune and forget the one who is the source of all that is good. We sometimes even think that we no longer need God, after all everything is going on fine. Some foolishly believe that all their success is due entirely to their own abilities, power, or business acumen, because they have forgotten where those gifts come from. The question is; can God trust you with wealth?

Definitely, the temptation is enormous for those of us who grew up in hardship. We can easily get caught up in the success and once-unimaginable prosperity. The clear danger for any impoverished person who enters his/her Promised Land is the danger of forgetting where they came from. Just a little food in the stomach will make yesterday's hunger seems years in the past. And just like for the Israelites, for us too, this admonition is very clear: never forget that it is God who gives us the power to get wealth.

GROW-UP, LEARN AND PERSEVERE

"EVERYONE IS THE ARCHITECT OF HIS OWN FORTUNE"

—Abbe Regnier

When I was a very little boy, I was driven by an ambitions needs to succeed. While my other friends played ball and cards, I was steeped in a desire to create my future and fulfill my dreams. My mum and I grew vegetables in our backyard. It was fun, but it was hard work. I would then sell the extra vegetables we couldn't eat for some extra cash which my mum would use to support the family in some other ways. Seeing me roaming all over the streets carrying a head tray of vegetables then was a common sight in our neighbourhood.

Once it was harvest season, I was out everyday, carrying those heavy trays up and down the streets of the military base where we lived. Sometimes I had my elder sister join me but sooner than later she grew too big for that business. When it was off harvest season we would switch from vegetables to selling either soft drinks or sugar cane. The weight of the head tray of vegetables and soft drinks pained my back and caused my head to ache. To the average person there it was just okros or pepsi on an head tray. But to the discerning eye there was far more than vegetables or soft drinks loaded in the head tray. There were the secret principles of greatness in the head tray. There was the lesson of going after what you wanted, the courage of knocking on the door, shouting on the streets, dealing with rejection sometimes, rudeness other times, arguing, urging and debating with prospective buyers, but still pressing towards your with a relentlessness that was stronger than a few insults could eradicate. And although those trays of vegetables and soft drinks were heavy, I persevered. All dreams are heaviest in infancy. If all that you carry is easy to handle, you will never develop your potential.

Yes I was brought-up carrying trays of vegetables. I was brought-up to carry my own weight. Just like an ant carrying a morsel of bread to his dwelling place, greatness is often dragged by persons who seem too small to carry what they believe but are far too stubborn to leave it behind. You must learn to be tenacious and relentless, to carry your own destiny even when you think it is too heavy, and to persevere through the pain. Today when I tell young men who have difficulty finding a job to create one, I do so because I learned as a little boy that if success doesn't come after you, you have to go after it.

An industrious spirit has no time to wait on glamour. Just as I went from selling vegetables to selling soft drink, it didn't matters what you are working with, it only matters where you are going and how relentless you pursued your dreams. It won't take long for you to notice God's blessings on you. Even if you don't think about the blessings at the time, you would later realize that Psalm chapter one verse three is right when it says, "whatsoever he doeth shall prosper". God blesses what you do, not what you think, dream or fantasize. God blesses what you do. In each of us lies a seed of greatness, a potential, and a gift. Your gift could be in your tenacity and entrepreneurial spirit. Your gift could be in dreams that stayed in your soul! Even when your eyes are awake you still dreamed. You are a daydreamer, a water—walker and a bridge-builder. If only you can trace down your gift and identify your dream, you'll have the power to get up and move on. Achievers start now. You cannot wait on opportunity. The opportunity I think is the breath in your body and the strength of your mind. If you use your gift wisely, there is no telling what you can do. But God only blesses what you do, remember! We must be doers. We must be people of action. It all boils down to your faith in the fact that you have the power to change what is hindering you.

The Bible says God gives us not wealth, but the power to get wealth. There is a big difference between the two. Too many people are sitting around or overstuffed, most will still be sitting there next year and the following year, with empty laps. A dream without a corresponding action aggregates the soul and leads to nothing. Put your dreams in your actions. Your actions will determine whether you are just a dreamer or an achiever. God will give you the power to get wealth, but you will have to take the power and get a plan and work the plan to make it happen. God gives us the capacity or means to get wealth. That power is in your will. It is in your talents. It is in your creativity.

Never you laugh at someone who has an idea. Ideas are the ingredients of change. All that we see around us are thoughts turned into physical reality. Have you ever stopped to realize that most money is made as the result of a good idea? What is your idea? What are you thinking? Whatever you are thinking, that is what you are creating in your life. When God gives you the power to get wealth, one of those powers so often ignored is a divine thought. If you have a brain, you can think and can come up with something of value to humanity.

Drop your brains on the ground and make money—that is the real definition of free enterprise. As people who believe in God, we have the added advantage of the spirit of God living within us. Who made everything that has been made and knows everything about all that was created, so why won't he give you the gift to come up with business ideas? Many of us are full of holy-Spirit-inspired creative ideas that have never been worked out into reality because we have failed to make and carry out a plan. These are the seeds of greatness many let rot on the ground of excuses. Of course there are challenges obstacles, but there are also rewards.

We all have talents. They are gifts from God, the manifestation of the Holy Spirit within us. My gift may be different from yours, but they have the same source. As a businessman, I am successful because I see and understand the capacity God has given me and am maximizing the moment.

You could be active in business and still have something else you do which is your passion. But most importantly, you have business success, which is the result of ones creativity and the source of financial success. Your success comes from working with the power that God has given you to generate wealth through the marketing of ideas. Creativity is the sources of wealth, and creativity comes from the creator. You must know and acknowledge that it is the Lord who gives all of us the power. But what will we do with that power He gives us? You also need to understand that you must take what He's put within and work it out. You have to shine a light on the untapped potentials that are lying dormant inside you. That creative idea He breathed into you will work if you work it.

KEY TO SUCCESS

The gift, talent or ability God gave you is your key to success. God did not give it to you for it to be put on display behind a showcase. He did not give it to you to waste. God gave you a gift to be poured out, used, and invested.

Jesus gave us a parable about talents. First let me define a parable as a story that tells a special lesson or truth. And in that parable he insisted that God gave everyone a talent. In his own words, "And unto one he gave five talents, to another two, and to another one; to every man according to his own ability..." Matthew 25:15. Your talent is your gift or ability and as you heard Jesus, every man has one or more and that it is based on your own ability. What exactly was the talent that is put inside of us by the creator meant to be used for and how was it meant to be used.

The answers are also contained in Jesus' words. In the book of Luke chapter nineteen, he said; "And he called his ten servants, and delivered to them ten talents, and said unto them, occupy till I come". Luke 19:13. As I said earlier, talent does not necessary mean money, money was used here just as an illustration. Now some other translation of the bible puts the phrase "occupy till I come" as "do business till I return". That means every man is supposed to use his/her talent to do business with it before Jesus comes back. If every man has a talent and we are supposed to do business with it, I wouldn't be stoned to death if I say life is business. A friend of mine puts it this way "life is commerce".

How was the talent put inside of us meant to be used is the last question. Also in the words of the great teacher; "And it came to pass, that when he was returned, having received the kingdom, then he commanded these servants to be called unto him, to whom he had given the talent, that he might know how much every man had gained by trading"—Luke 19:15. Did you see that—by trading—is the means by which you are supposed to use-up your talent. By trading also means by doing business. Life is business not pleasures. For pleasures only comes through toil.

"LIFE, FACULTIES, PRODUCTION—IN OTHER WORD INDIVIDUALITY, LIBERTY, PROPERTY—THIS IS MAN"

—Frederic Bastiat.

A man must first know who he is, what he has and what he is willing to invest. You must also know why you are investing and what you hope to achieve in the pursuit of such an investment. It is not enough to just be investing; you must know your strength and weaknesses so as to be able to handle your decision—making process better. Now this is important before you even take the first step towards making your financial fortune because every decision you take in life will either build you or break you.

By knowing who you are and where you stand on the queue, you can easily design a plan of action, chart a path, determine what direction to take, you must know what you're willing to give and how much you hope to get out of life to be really satisfied. You can regularly change your bar of excellence based on the new information you acquire. Since they are your goals, it doesn't make much difference they were only changed for positive and productive reasons. Isn't it? The most important thing is that you have a focused mind and you're only changing to add more colours to your life.

LEARNING BY THE ROPES

"THE BUSINESSMAN, THE ACTING MAN, IS ENTIRELY ABSORBED IN ONE TASK ONLY, TO TAKE ADVANTAGE OF

ALL THE MEANS AVAILABLE FOR THE IMPROVEMENT OF FUTURE CONDITIONS"

—Ludwig Von Mises

The million-dollar question is how did all the great people know what they were to do. I believe the easiest way to learn is by the ropes. That is, looking at the lives of the highly successful businessmen and pulling out common denominators so that you can logically analyze it and apply it to your life. Now if we look at the lives of highly successful entrepreneurs, one major characteristic stands out over and over again. It is not their simple enjoyment for doing business but rather it is a deep heartfelt desire, drive, program and urge to succeed.

Critically, most of the successful people in the past and present, where from very poor families, disadvantaged individuals or immigrants who arrive at a foreign land broke without a dime. They needed any job that was available. They needed money to feed first. At that phase in their lives, working hard to earn money to eat was a matter of survival. In those early stages though, it takes long stretched hours of hard work to be able to afford the basic necessities of life. These men had great value for their hard earned money than the other folks who just wakes up to a pinned money claimed by inheritance or winning from a lottery/pool.

Anyone who aspires to be like these great businessmen must be driven by the urge to make money. Set targets for yourself with a time frame, have the gusto and determination to hit the target. Truth is that, it is better to die for what you believe than to live for nothing. Spending all of your life to hit those targets, often, will build our faith, spirituality, strength, diligence and sense of purpose. You will by this facts completely escape being caught up in the mini-tie of a mundane existence

This kind of determination will help you to have a saving purse no matter how small your income is. At least a little money is better that no money at all. And as you watch your saving purse bulge, it reinstates in your mind that you are actually drifting towards success. It will keep in you the desire you started out with and reinforce it as you progress in life. You will begin to perceive the aroma of success and begin to taste its sweetness. Because of your savings, you will feel happy, to such, success has never tasted so sweet.

As time progresses, things get better, increases faster, and becomes more evident, growth is now noticeable. You begin to more from faith to faith and from glory to glory. The need for survival gradually transforms to the need for success. And then need for even accomplishing more and more.

As you monitor your day-to-day progress, your mind becomes alert to all the profits that are visible or invisibly available. As a result, the businessman will not look at any circumstance with the same eyes of the man seeking pleasures. The business mastermind doesn't think negatively. It is an optimistic mind. On the other hand, the pleasure seeker is a pessimist. The optimist sees the positive side in every situation, the pessimist always sees the negative sides. While the optimistic business-mind sees opportunity in every problem, the pessimistic pleasure—seeker sees problem in every opportunity. The successful business mind didn't look at things the traditional way they've been doing it for ages, he looked at things to come up with solutions, that is what we call 'positive thinking'.

Averagely, the excellent thinker opts into jobs that others wouldn't do, since those were the available ones at his disposal he takes them. This is the same reasoning that pushes them into a business area that nobody else has ventured. In the long run, the successful business serves the need of the consuming public in the market place which has had a great and intense desire of such product for a long time now. These businesses identify a craving need in the market, and they go all out to satisfy that need in the market. Of course as they go all out to satisfy such a need in its best way possible at the moment, the consumers are willing to pay for it. We would be right to say that, the greatest businesses traded where others dreaded!

LORD OF THE MARKET PLACE

"EVERY ENTERPRISE IS BUILT BY WISE PLANNING, IT BECOMES STRONG THROUGH THE USE OF COMMON SENSE AND PROFITS WONDERFULLY BY KEEPING ABREAST OF THE FACTS"

—Proverbs 24:3-4

All successful business strives on facts. Just like proverbs put it in the amplified version, I call it the almighty formula for business success. The business masterminds do not just begin to produce because they thought that people would need their product, or did they produce and began praying that some days, some kind of demand for their products might erupt! No. They knew and knew vividly well that the consumers were n dear need of their products or services before they even began producing anything. To the business mastermind, self-satisfaction is not a reason to produce but rather consumer satisfaction is their most consuming passion. They reached their profit advantage by serving the consumers and properly meeting up to the demands voiced by thousands and millions of individuals in the market place while making their own cool wealth and evolving, their dreams.

Good-news is that, you too can have a shoot at the big goal. Because the highest flying industries of yester-years are in troubled waters today. What looked like the best option some years back, today might well just seem out of place? They say taste change, time changes everything, there is a changing process for everything of course; ideas, producers, consumers. You don't need to get coca-cola's magic formula to dominate too, all you need to do is create your own magic formula and have your own brand name to make an impact, like them. Add one more style to the market place which no doubt is far more complex today. And the uncertainty and complexity of the market will create for any individual a great chance to grab an opportunity for his/her product, service or a combination of both to satisfy the consumers yearning desire and so they are willing to pay for it.

You will also need to know that the more complex and uncertain the market gets, the more difficult it will be for central agencies and giant firms to have a direct impact. This is the reason why I am prescribing the free enterprise system for African countries to adopt now. Our governments can do very little, than sit and desire to do good and better the lives of it's citizen by trying to improve the economy. They really can't change the economy, they have been too cool. But watch what happens if businesses of the state goes into the hands of private individuals and private corporations. You know what will happen? Everyone will be thinking, they will want to grow, expand and make good profit. Success will be won on merit. The free market place is with out doubt the best way to decentralize all the centrally controlled governments and agencies of African countries and still these governments will maintain their firm grip on the society's culture, laws and governing power. It will affect everyone from the competing producer to consuming public. It will give the common man some powers and create a sense of patriotism. Good still, today's businessman is lucky to live in this nuclear age with it's multitude of opportunities and then the African businessman is the luckiest to be around the continent at this time that the wave of economic revolution is plowing towards her. Hurray!

It's Africa's time to rule the world's economy. No doubt the future of Africa's economy is being restored and we are about experiencing an excellent shift of economic powers. In a world's economy dominated by giant corporations from the western countries, it is inspirational to watch the dynamic process of the market continually knock down inefficient giant firms and replace them with up and coming business who are out-performing these world leaders. The criteria of efficiency and the changing flux of time gives every advantage to the new corporation or individual who has vision and insight to recognize an opportunity and the motivation, determination, courage, diligence and will to act.

"GOD BLESSES THE ACTIONS OF MEN AND WOMEN WHO ARE NOT AFRAID TO MAKE A MOVE"

—Bishop T. D Jakes

This giant multinationals lack the information's and flexibility single enterprising individuals have. The quick, agile, mobile, new and alert small-scale entrepreneur can make a major financial incursion in the big world's market. That is why I'm convinced that younger visioners arising from Africa will take the world by storm.

Honestly, it is not too difficult to find a niche for yourself in the market place the way those elite entrepreneurs make it look. A good idea turns opportunity into fortune. The real problem is how to locate that seed of fortune and once located what to do with it. Once the seed has been identified, then the process begins. It takes time though, but when well planted, nurtured and properly taken care of it grows to maturity and to a full size tree initially and finally a forest.

Remember that back woods Georgia drug clerk called Asa Candler? He gave his life savings to a country doctor who was holding a charred black kettle of viscous liquid and a slip of paper containing the syrup's formula. Candler transformed his five hundred dollars investment into a soft drink that came to be named coca-cola.

To all the young enthusiastic thinking fellows out there, make hay while the sun is still shining. You know of course that the way you make your bed is the way you'll lie on it. Invest in business today and reap an ever-increasing flow of income and leaving behind an enduring legacy even long after you leave the scene. Make generations to come be grateful to God for creating you in their lineage. If you spend your money on high technologies, porch cars and houses, cloths and the likes of it without investing a substantial amount into your future, sooner than later you will become unable to maintain the high standard of living you have forcefully set for yourself. It's a masquerade! So before you make your choice in life, think through. Read this book and others that will motivate your entrepreneurial spirit, associate with people of like minds and with good advice, make war. We are at it again—I challenge the faithful to become practical, and the practical to become faithful. One must compliment the other.

"YOUR SUCCESS AND HAPPINESS LIE IN YOU, EXTERNAL CONDITIONS ARE THE ACCIDENTS OF LIFE"

—Helen Keller.

Most of all, success is a life-long process of learning. Learning from others, learning from your failures, learning by doing. Everything you know you need to learn first. People are always looking for the secrets to success. There are lots of A-B-C and 1-2-3 books on the bookshelves. Experts share their formulas for making money and getting rich. CEO's and captains of industries write about their experiences on how they made it to the top.

I personally believe that the secret to success is that there are no secrets to success. The formula for wealth is that there is no formula. If you think this book was going to tell you some secrets or share with you some formulas, I'm sure by now you know it won't. I don't claim to have a secret or a formula. I simply wish to share with you some opinion of my and of those we often tag successful.

When we look at the lives of those who have gone ahead of us there is usually so much to learn. What they did in certain circumstances how they did it, where they did it and what they were saying in the pursuit of their desired goal, in the hopes that they may help us in some ways through similar or even strange circumstances. In the following chapters, you will read the stories of some of these men. I also include bits and pieces, sayings to serve as advise that might be helpful to you in making your decisions. But, frankly, they are not secrets and they are not guaranteed formulas or recipes. They are just basic ingredients. You have to put them in the bowl of your life and stir. The simple truth is that success is something you dream of and then something you work for—that depends on you, not on me and not on this book. The ball is in your court, play it the best way you can.

7

'HEROES ON PARADE'

HEROES ON PARADE

To understand how hard work and an entrepreneurial spirit can accomplish great things, it is helpful to begin by learning something about those who have gone ahead of us and had succeeded one way or the other either as entrepreneur, businessmen, and industrialist or as professionals in their field. It did however, work for them because of a free system. They saw needs and worked to fill them.

As much as I could with the information's available to me I will be giving dates, figures, who did what, where, when, why and how certain breakthroughs were achieved. Those that failed at certain times, why they failed so that we can avoid it. Those that succeeded, what lead to their success, so we can learn from it. Those that stayed long in business, why they stayed long so we too can stay long in business. No doubt, we are inspired by those who had the courage, persistence, or genius to be entrepreneurs and innovators when the conditions were tougher and the opportunities fewer. These people, from the ancient past, deserve to be called entrepreneurs because in an important sense they are the distant relatives and "spiritual parents" of modern entrepreneurialism. Hard working innovators have contributed immeasurably to our world and created opportunities for generations that followed them. So who were some of those "entrepreneurs"

THOMAS ALVA EDISON

Thomas Edison was born in Milan, Ohio, February 11, 1847. perhaps, the greatest inventor the world has ever known, had only three months of formal education and was considered by his school teacher to be retarded, incapable or not able to learn. By the time he died, though, he had filed over a thousand patents and was a very wealthy man.

Edison perfected and patented everything from the first phonograph player in 1877 to the first practical light bulb in 1879. He set up the first electricity-distribution company, contributed to the development of the movie camera and projector, and made important improvements in the telephone, telegraph and typewriter.

The light bulb is a good example of the entrepreneurial spirit alive and well in our early history. Perhaps you thought that Edison invented the light bulb when a light suddenly went on in is head. But in his time this expression would apply only if it were a gaslight! Infact, Edison invented the light bulb not in a flash of insight, but over a period of time after trials and errors—in short in a very systematic way. He would later say, "I failed nine hundred times trying to invent the electric bulb, but I knew nine hundred ways the electric bulb would not work". His approach to invention is one of the earliest illustrations of a process that has come to be known as research and development.

Edison had six rules for invention. Even if you don't think you are ever going to invent something as world—changing as the electric bulb, just look closely how these rules work: you could of course use them to see your own dreams come true.

1. Set a goal and stick to it

2. Figure out the steps you have to go through to complete the invention and follow them.

3. Keep good records of your progress

4. Share your results with fellow workers

5. Be sure that everyone working on the project has a clear definition of their responsibilities

6. Record all your results for later analysis

For quite a while now, scientist all over have used this systematic approach to solve problems. However, surprisingly, Edison adapted this approach to invent things for the market place he was an entrepreneur as much as he was an inventor. He wasn't interested in making things that didn't sell—he was interested in knowing what people wanted to buy. Therefore, he was very thorough in doing his marketing homework well. Edison's team of inventors became the world's first industrial research laboratory—a uniquely American institute at the time. His lab was the first of several others to follow including the Bell Laboratory and General Electric—GE.

Less I forget, when Edison was busy developing a way to distribute electricity to power his new light bulbs because he discovered it was hard to sell light bulbs when no one has any electricity to fire 'em up! In 1882 he established a small power distribution system in New York. This was the first electric 'utility' ever set up to serve household. Though it was a success, Edison had a few problems at first. The evidence is found on almost every electrical appliance you've ever plugged in. Did you ever notice that most of them say, "For use with 110—volts only"?

Why was it 110 volts? Edison's first power—generating system couldn't maintain sufficient power throughout the system. The people near the power station had light bulbs burning brightly, but by the end of the line, things were pretty dim. So Edison got complaints. So like any good entrepreneur—he wanted to sell lots of light bulbs—he then decided to increase up the power from 100 to 110 volts, remarkable you would say! This new standard stuck, even when distribution systems became sophisticated enough to overcome the original problem.

"THE ABILITY TO INVENT IS 2%, INSPIRATION AND 98% PERSPIRATION

—Thomas Edison.

Just think for a moment the changes one invention brought about—electricity. Vast new areas were opened up for entrepreneurs and consumers alike—not only in telephones and light bulbs but radio, television, computer and thousands of other products.

WILBUR AND ORVILLE WRIGHT

Wilbur Wright was born on April 16, 1867 on a farm new castle. And Orville Wright was born August 19, 1871 in Dayton, Ohio. So two brothers were born—one in Indiana and the other in Ohio—who invented and built the first successful airplane on Dec 17, 1903. They made the world first flight.

They went into the bicycle business together, they did well as bicycle entrepreneurs, but their interest and what made them famous was aeronautics.

After several years of eagerly reading the latest research that has been made on the problem of flight, in 1899 the two brothers began to work on some solutions themselves. By 1903 their efforts paid—off by the result of the first manned flight. Having built many gliders, the brothers had become the world's most experienced gilder pilots, with more than a thousand successful flights made.

These experiences led them to an understanding of a fundamental problem of flights, which was control. After devising a way to maneuver their craft in the air, they added a lightweight engine of their own design and flew into the air, the rest is history. They were granted the first patent on the airplane in 1906. Their total investment had been about one thousand dollars.

ALEXANDER GRAHAM BELL

Alexander Graham Bell was an American born in Scotland in the year 1847. He is of no doubt one of the spectacular example of how quickly free enterprise developed new products and inventions in the last part of the nineteenth century. He patented the telephone in February 1876 and exhibited his new invention at the centennial exposition in Philadelphia that same year. It was an instant hit. At the time, the biggest communications company in the United States was the Western Union Telegraph Company—Bell offered the rights to his new invention to western union for a hundred thousand dollars—of course the offer was promptly refused.

The next year Bell formed his own corporation, which was an immediate success. That company eventually became the American Telephone and Telegraph Company—AT&T—I'm sure you must have heard of it. From the month of March to November of 1879, just within eight month, stock in Bell's company went from sixty—five dollars a share to over a thousand dollars (by this time, western union were biting their figures), by 1822; New York and Chicago were connected by telephone. By the time Bell died in 1922, the telephone was common throughout the country. It went from being a new invention to a regular household item with remarkable speed no one could believe. For sure, it made Bell very wealthy.

JAMES WATT

James Watt, an Englishman believes that people could learn how to do things through books and perhaps even more important, they learned to be innovators by combining others' ideas with their own. By so doing, he filled a very great need in history and industrial development. He designed the world's first practical steam engine, patented in1769. Improving on a crude, steam—powered pumping device he had seen. Watt made some major modifications, added some entirely new features and converted an impractical curiosity into a valuable tool. It might be difficult for us to imagine how great this invention was. During the time of Watt's there was no electric power—the electric moter wasn't invented then. Neither were there any gasoline engines.

If you wanted to do any heavy work, like grind grain or run a cloth mill, you had to do it with waterpower. This was of great inconvenience, to say the least, and severely limited the amount of work that can be done.

However, watt's invention was almost single-handly responsible for the development of the industrial revolution. With a practical source of power, all kind of things could be done. Soon, entrepreneurs of every kind thought of ways to put this new power source to work. What a breakthrough!

TS'AI LUN

One of the most remarkable story of an entrepreneur/innovator I like is that of a Chinese official named Ts'ai Lun who invented paper in A.D. 105. Before Lun's invention, almost everything was written on bamboo. The made books very heavy and clumsy. Chinese scholars needed a wagon to carry around just a few books.

Ts'ai lun's invention was recognized immediately for it's great value. He was promoted by the emperor, made an aristocrat, and become wealthy. This invention changed china dramatically and eventually the rest of the world. Books become more available and, in turn, they spread learning throughout the country. Why remarkable? I said that because can you just imagine how it would have looked like if we were still writing a bamboos.

JOHANNES GUTENBERG

About 1400, in the city of Mainz, an innovative German goldsmith, Johannes Gutenberg, perfected a series of inventions that made modern printing possible. Gutenberg invented a practical way of making and using movable type, which made feasible the printing of a wide variety of books with speed and accuracy.

Although, notable events had taken place between the time of Ts'ai Lun and Gutenberg, the pace of progress in the world speed up tremendously after Gutenberg's invention. The development of printing was one of the most important events in the making of our modern world.

In one sense, printing made entrepreneurship possible for every single person, because information could now be easily transmitted. How-to-do books were among the very first to be printed. They covered every imaginable subject from metallurgy to medicine, from good building techniques to good manners. People learned how to do things through book, and perhaps even more important, they learned to be innovators by combining others' ideas with their own. A point I earlier said James Watt implored and even Michael Faraday—one of the greatest experimental scientists of all times.

NIKOLAUS OTTO

Nikolaus Otto is a German Inventor and one of the many entrepreneurs who have had a significant impact on our daily lives during the last century till now. Tagged as the unknown patron saint of our 'car culture' Otto invented the first practical automobile engine in the year 1876.

He had a junior employee named Gottlieb Daimler, who got together a few years later with a friend, Carl Benz. They started building cars using engines based on Otto's design and decide to name the cars after the daughter of a dealer who sold their cars a girl named Mercedes.

Like the electric motor, the internal—combustion engine was soon used in all kinds of small factories and shops. Almost immediately after its invention it was being used to power pumps, sewing machines, printing presses, saws—all kinds of things. It was big and bulky by today's standards, but it was still an improvement over steam power. How big?

Otto built a special racing engine in 1901 that weighed a thousand pounds and produced forty horsepower. A common Volkswagen "beetle" engine of the 1960s produced forty horsepower and could be picked up by two average men. A modern motorcycle engine now produces much power and can be picked by only one person. That means competition among capitalist entrepreneurs fostered these rapid advances.

Cars created entrepreneurial opportunities for millions of people across the globe. Cars required a lot of raw materials and people to produce them. These included steel, glass, chrome, rubber, wire, paint, and upholstery fabric—all kinds of things. These cars required roads, bridges and tunnels. Mechanics were needed to keep them running, gas and filling stations to fuel them, an insurance agent to insure them—the list is endless.

The mobility that people enjoyed in their cars created some whole new industries: motels and resorts, roadside café's, trailers and car parks etc. The automobile introduced a new culture to the world.

As we have seen, most of the consumer products that we take for granted are very recent creations. The entrepreneurial spirit is alive and working in us. And the pace of innovations and change has accelerated tremendously in the twentieth century. Almost all of those thousand of products that the free enterprise system manufactures so efficiently are the result of what has happened in the past one hundred years. Africa has missed out in the twentieth century; does she want to miss out in the twenty-first century? God forbid!

THE BUSINESS MASTERMINDS

Our schools higher institutions and universities are frankly speaking made up of educated paupers. You see highly placed lecturers and professors dying in poverty and lack—I say this with all due respect to our institutions of higher learning, I know they will forgive me.

The point I'm bringing out is this; more than ninety percent of the wealthiest people on earth, ironically, come out from the group you could easily tag uneducated. They were from families of immigrants, refugees, were poor and disadvantaged.

Why then, and how did they make it to the top of the business world? Could it be that the scholars who have been taught theoretically and also in turn teach others can't successfully apply the knowledge at their disposal to strike it rich? And unlearnered novices are breaking the records of wealth everywhere around the world.

Well I think this is the reason: just like you don't teach a man the lessons of life, but he learns it through various factors including learning from others' by observing their successes or mistakes, from experience, from circumstances, from certain conditions and situations—the techniques for becoming wealthy can't be taught at all in the classroom. Inspiration, motivation, desire and a strong will to do something great are the factors that ignite the flame of success.

Now, one of the surest way to ignite your appetite for great achievement is to peep into, get some help and imitate those who through patience, faith and hard work did become successful. Among which are most of the business people that made America one of the richest country in the world by the simple ideology of free enterprise—Henry Ford, Andrew Carnegie, Ray Kroc, and John D. Rockefeller, Asa Candler just to mention but a few.

You can build your financial empire working wisely. First for a salary and then for yourself—when you've built your own enterprise. All of these business masterminds applied a simple tactics.

They went after profit possibilities. And as they did, they looked for opportunities, recognized them and then got their breakthroughs. Initially though it didn't matter much which line of business they doubled into, but had their vision in mind and maintained their big—picture—perspective. As they moved from one end to another, they gave their lives more focus. They knew that the most important thing was how to create wealth given a set of economic conditions—favorable or unfavorable

ANDREW CARNEGIE
* The King of Steel *

Andrew whose father was a poor Scottish immigrant was only thirteen years old when he first arrived the United States in 1848. Of course he arrived without a dime, but he had a dream. Sooner than later, he got himself a job and was earning one dollar-twenty cent a week to help support his family. He later progressed in his job as well as income so that by two years time he was making three dollars a week as an operator in a telegraph company. Still progressing in life though little by little, he was earning six dollars a week with a railroad company at the age of nineteen.

One major attribute of highly successful people like Andrew Carnegie is the ability to recognize your breakthrough when it first appears—looking like heavy responsibility. You need to know that responsibility is the price of greatness; no irresponsible man has a future. So Carnegie was quick to recognize his major break when it first appeared in the form of 'responsibility' and 'work'. He was made the secretary to the superintendent of the then Pittsburgh railroad.

Now his boss by name Scott, a military Colonel was one of the most informed personalities about almost every business that was growing in Pittsburgh. With quality information, therefore, from his new boss and some of his guts, Andrew Carnegie at that tender young age bought interest in a small Pennsylvania oil company without paying a dime. Using a written agreement to pay in one year with his dividend from the stocks, Carnegie made his first major investment in life.

He did actually make very small money in the long run. With this money, Carnegie used it as the capital to invest in some local stock right there at Pittsburgh based on the recommendation he got from his boss.

And all this while, Carnegie remained Scott's secretary for close to ten years. And in 1864, he was called upon to occupy Scott's sit at the railroad; he was still twenty-eight years of age. Then, in the following year he still made another major investing-putting in about eight thousand nine hundred and twenty dollars for a seventeen percent interest in the iron city forge company.

Then 1864 passed by, Carnegie still the superintendent at the railroad had also acquired some vital information's of his own. For instance, he knew that steel was ore durable compared to iron which was then used for railroad because iron was quit soft. At that time, steel was too expensive, but Carnegie knew that the future of the railroad lies on steel.

And just according to his calculations, plans for the western railroads where been drawn up and of course the demands for iron rails was so high that even iron city forge company was selling every single production of product. Of course allowed other manufacturers to come in and the cost of iron to fall. The steel manufacturers began to approach their opportunities. At this point now, investors knew it, so did Carnegie, but instead he continued with his iron manufacturing and later formed the keystone bridge company. And only after four years of buying the company on paper, did he eventually pay for it with the profit he had realized in his period from the company.

And just about that time too, the Pennsylvania railroad needed iron bridges and then Carnegie made sure that all the orders was received by keystone bridge company to supply all the irons they could supply for the iron bridges.

What else for Carnegie, a recession set in after the civil war had ended. Though he utilized every opportunity in those bad circumstances, he finally got the survival breakthrough when he emerged as the sole owner of iron city Forge Company. So by logic in 1873, Andrew Carnegie was now a multimillionaire and was on his way to become the king of steel.

Though he was not the first to verge into the steel business Carnegie was very calculative enough to verge into it at the approval of those who showed its profitability. He strategically gathered information's from insiders before investing with little or no money of his in cash. He was very calculative, he did grasp every given opportunity for his personal benefit and generated ideas and intuition for every given set of situation with only one major thing in mind "how to make profit and make money from it". He viewed every opportunity through a financial microscope with the external conditions notwithstanding. Though he dabbled into various sectors of the system on his way up, he was still much focused and scrutinized every new set of ideas. He first became bobbin boy for one dollar twenty cents a week remember and then telegraph operator for three dollars a week. Moved unto a railroad worker and became a secretary to Colonel Scott where he learned a lot about business and venturing to its dept.

Carnegie knew nothing about the production and technicality aspect of the business he was venturing into, it didn't even matter what business he got into, all he wanted was to be an entrepreneur, a free enterpriser, a capitalist, a producer—all he wanted was to do business. So even when Carnegie knew little about the technical process of making steel, he became the king of steel.

HENRY FORD
* Ford Motors *

Henry Ford was born on July 30, 1863 in Dearborn, Michigan, USA. His father was a farmer and didn't see any reason for his son to continue going to school. In fact, when Henry finished primary school, his father judged that he would be more useful on the farm, instead of wearing out the seat of his pants on a school bench; as a result, Ford was soon introduced to the hard manual labor of farming.

The first thing Henry Ford remembered owning were odds and ends of metal, which he always converted into tools. While other boys of his age spent their days playing in the field, Henry occupied most of his time in a small workshop that his father had given him permission to set up in a shed on the family farm. When he was twelve years old, Henry Ford had an experience that was to transform and direct his life.

"The biggest event of those early years was a meeting with a road engine about eight miles out of Detroit. One day when we were driving to town, I was about twelve years old. I remember that engine as though I had seen it only yesterday, for it was the first vehicle other than horse—drawn that I had ever seen. The engine had stopped to let us pass with our horses and I was off the wagon and talking to the engineer before my father, who was driving, knew what I was up to. It was that engine which took me into automotive transportation. I tried to make models of it and some years later I did make one that ran very well, but from the time I saw that road engine as a boy of twelve right to today, my great interest has been in making a machine that would travel the road"

"Interesting work is easy and I am always certain of results" was his formula. He would become a machinist's apprentice for the Dry-dock engine works. His father strongly disapproved of this, since he naturally viewed his son as a good strong back for his farm. He gave his son up for lost.

America, on the other hand, had just found one of it's greatest industrialists. "When I was not cutting timber, I was working on the gas engine—learning what they were and how they acted. I read everything I could find, but the greatest knowledge comes from my work".

His efforts and perseverance were not in vain. In 1892, when he was twenty nine years old, seventeen years after having seen that famous road engine and having vowed that he would one day achieve his dream, he put the finishing touches on his first automotive engine. It took seventeen long years and countless sacrifices before he finally achieved his goal. Genius, so they say is infinite patience. Success also demands patience. Those who are tempted to give up after a few month or a few years should be encouraged by this man's tenacity.

The residents of Detroit were probably as surprised by the sight of a young man straddling this first petrol 'buggy' as they would have been by visiting extraterrestrials. "it was considered to be something of a nuisance, for it made a racket and it scared horses. Also it blocked traffic. For if I stop my machine any where in town a crowed was around it before I could start up again. If I left it alone even for a minute some inquisitive person always tried to run it. Finally, I had to carry a chain and chain it to a lamp post whenever I left it anywhere".

"It was not at all my idea to make cars in any such petty fashion. I was looking ahead to production, but before that could come I had to have something to produce. It does not pay to hurry". During this time he continued working for the Detroit Edison Company. If Ford wanted a position, he would have to give up his research on petrol engines and devote himself entirely to electrical energy. In short, he was being asked to give up his dream. In exchange, he was being offered material security and a guaranteed future. Most people would have jumped at this offer. After all a bird in hand worth two in the bush. Most people need for security is so great that they would be prepared to sacrifice their most precious dreams for it. It didn't take Henry Ford long to make up his mind. He preferred trying his luck and devoting himself to realizing this dream; the mass production of petrol—propelled vehicle. Once again in the history of mankind, one man was going to prove that he could prove the skepticism of an entire nation unfounded. "It was make or break," said Henry Ford.

"I resigned, determined never to take orders". On August 15 1899, Ford left the Edison Company, completely penniless. He now had to prove wrong the assumption that the automobile was a rich man's plaything. No 'serious' businessman in Detroit would have invested penny in such a risky venture. Nevertheless, Ford managed to persuade a few enterprising businessmen to back him in the construction of petrol—propelled machine and founded the Detroit Automobile Company.

A conflict inevitable grew between Ford and his backers. Ford resigned. This bitter experience, however, had not destroyed Ford's convictions. It did teach him a simple principle, however: to make a fortune, you have to be independent and have your own business firmly in hand. 'It is nice to plan to do one's work in office hours, to take up the work in the morning, to drop it in the evening and not have a care until the next morning. It is perfectly possible to do that if one is so constituted as to be willing through all of one's life to accept direction, to be an employee, possibly a responsible employee, but not a director or manager of anything".

He believed that few people will be bold enough to launch their own product, and that they will simple continue to copy his. Ford always told himself: 'why not do better? 'And that's exactly what he resolved to do. Ford's business boomed, and his cars were soon reputed to be the most solid and dependable ever built. It was in 1903, that he designed two vehicles that were specially built for racing and called them '999' and 'Arrow'. Ford won the race by half a mile. Every body now knew that Ford built the fastest cars. Spurred on by his success, Ford decided to gamble everything by founding the Ford Motor Company. He became it's vice—president, chief engineer, chief mechanic, floor supervisor and managing director. His reasoning was simple; it was better to strike while the iron was still hot. He had to take the plunge from such great publicity. It was now or never. He rented a bigger workshop and got down to work with the help of a few associates.

After only five years of operation, the Ford Motor Company had 1,908 employees on it's payroll, owned it's own factory, and was producing 6,181 cars a year which were sold both in America and in Europe. The little boy who had once seen a road engine and sworn that he was going to build a self—propelled machine had realized his dream. He had become a millionaire. Yet, Henry Ford was not a man to say, I'm successful; I now earn a lot of money! Now is the time to stop". Instead he said "I can entirely sympathize with the desire to quit a life of activity and retire to a life of ease. I have never felt the urge myself but I can comprehend what it is—although I think that a man who retires ought to get out of business entirely. There is a disposition to retire and retain control. It was, however, no part of my plan to do any thing of that sort. I regarded our progress merely as an invitation to do more".

"If I had followed the general opinion of my associates, I should have kept the business as it was, put our funds into a fine administrative building, tried to make bargain with competitors that seemed too active, made new designs from time to time to catch the fancy of the public, and generally have passed into the position of a quite, respectable citizen with a quite respectable business". But Henry Ford saw much further than this and his vision was much, much bigger.

"I refuse to recognize that there are impossibilities. I cannot discover that any one knows enough about anything on this earth definitely to say what is and what is not possible. If some man, calling himself an authority, says that this or that cannot be done then a horde of unthinking follower's starts the chorus: it can't be done". For Henry Ford, the word impossible did not exist in the English language.

Henry Ford was one of the first to create a mechanized assembly—line system. By this very fact, he became the father of industrial robotics. According to him it was necessary to bring the work to the worker and not the other was around. This vision of things was going to upset the entire notion of productivity and human labor. His factory was to become the most modern in the world. Body parts suspended in mid air by enormous hooks were sent to assembly in the exact order assigned to them. The result was astonishing. The ten hours it normally took to assemble all the motor parts were reduced to five hours because of the assemble line. This small time mechanics idea was visionary, and his famous model T became such a success that Ford began opening up factories throughout the world. Ford factories were soon building 4,000 cars a days. When he died in 1947, Henry Ford, who had never worried about money, except to finance his dream, was a billionaire, which in those days was an astronomical feat.

Ford motors never stopped growing by 1960 it was considered the second largest enterprise in the world. By 1970, the company employed 432,000 people and had a wage fund of 3.5 billion dollars!

"Everything is possible, faith is the substance of things hoped for the evidence of things not seen". This succinct and deeply optimistic formula concluded Henry Ford's autobiography. These last words are a kind of spiritual legacy, and the fact that he spoke of faith is not at all by chance. All of his life and work proof that, for a person motivated by unshakable faith, everything is possible.

RAY KROC
* Mc Donald's *

"I HAVE ALWAYS BELIEVED THAT EVERY MAN CREATES HIS OWN HAPPINESS AND IS RESPONSIBLE FOR HIS OWN PROBLEMS".

Almost everyone in America has eaten a hamburger and French fries at one time or another. But to become rich selling them becomes the dream of Ray Kroc, the promoter of Mc Donald's Hamburger chain.

Ray Kroc, at age seventeen, worked at a soda fountain while in school. Saving his money, he went into the music store business, his first. The business did poorly and Ray sold out. He sold coffee beans and also sold novelties door to door. He worked as a cashier for a while.

As a student in school, Ray was highly attracted to debating classes. He did not care for reading much and dislike the slow progress of school. Ray was more of a man of action. Always a dreamer Ray was constantly imagining himself in different situations and figuring out what he would do. He was even called Danny Dreamer. But he loved work and worked at something whenever possible. Later, he was to say that "work is the hamburger in the meat of life".

He learned to play the piano as a child and used his musical ability to supplement his income as a salesman more than once. He even played in a bordello for one night but never went back when he found out what it was. Taking to the piano naturally, he played at dime—a—dance pavilions, on a ferry boat and also in an illegal club during prohibition. Having to share the tips, most of which he generated, he soon learned that by handling things differently, he could make more money by playing special requests and by playing serenading duos with the violinist when the rest of the band was on break.

Playing the piano for radio stations also brought him into the position of interviewing different people for the shows. Two men he hired were later to become the famous "Amos and Andy".

Ray started selling paper cups for Lilly cups when he was age twenty, the same year he married his first wife Ethel. It was to be three years later before Ray started to make his mark as a paper cup salesman. Since the paper cup business was slow in the north during winter, Ray would go to Florida in search of other work. He sold under waters property in the 20's real estate boom in Florida and worked difficult hours at night playing the piano. At age twenty-three he purchased his first new car because of his success selling paper cups.

Ray's father died in 1930 after losing his holdings in the real estate speculation boom that ended in the 29 crashes. This was the same year that Ray had captured his first large account, the Walgreen Drug Store chain from this account he went on to close sales at U.S. Steel, creameries and closed accounts at swift and Armour.

The merger of Lilly and Tulip Cup Companies in 1929 was an opportunity that Ray had seen; he had more lines to sell. He had also become a sales manager with around fifteen men working under him. He was a delight in seeing his men learn the ropes and become good sales men. Ray was to experience many detours before taking off with Mc Donald's, but he treated all of them as learning phase. The paper cup business led him into the multimixer business, which eventually led to Mc Donald's Hamburgers.

In his paper cup sales travels he had encountered a man named Earl Prince who had opened what were called prince castle ice cream parlors. It was prince who invented the multimixer. Seeing the opportunity of selling multimixers all over the country, Kroc immediately went to work. Two large obstacles were to stand in his way to success in selling multimixers. One was the sixty-eight thousand dollars buyout price to get exclusive distributor right for multimixer. Overcoming this adversity was to pay off later in his dealings in running Mc Donald's. Although World War II had temporarily ended his multimixer business because copper was being used for the war effort, Ray sold a malted milk product and managed to pay off his debt. When the war ended, Ray went back to selling multimixers and his business soon started rolling.

Five thousand multimixers a year was a good year for him and one year he sold eight thousand. Generating a large volume of business brought him his first and long time business associate, June Martiono. Ray desperately needed a bookkeeper and even though June had no book—keeping experience, he hired her basing his choice on the presence of her character. June was later to become secretary and treasurer of Mc Donald.

It was in the early 50's that Ray Kroc saw that he had to find a new product to sell. Multimixer sales were no longer booming. And it was the people who had been calling him to buy multimixers because of the once that they had seven in operation in a take-out restaurant in California that led Ray eventually to the Mc Donald's store there. Taking off for San Bernardino, a semi-desert town, Kroc was not expecting the experience that was soon to propel him to tremendous business. He went to find out why he was getting so many multimixer referrals from this one location. What he found was opportunity. But it was his keen business sense that enabled him see it.

The year was 1954. Ray Kroc was fifty-two years old. He was still "green and growing" as he calls it. Two brothers Mac and Dick Mc Donald had converted a conventional, yet successful, restaurant to a take-out restaurant. The new store was a masterpiece of simplicity and efficiency. Their only products, hamburgers and cheeseburgers, were so delicious that they drew all kinds of people from everywhere. The hamburgers were fifteen cent! The smoothness, cleanliness and rapid service of the whole operation so impressive Kroc that he immediately entered into a leasing arrangement with the Mc Donald's brothers.

"THINK SMALL AND YOU WILL STAY SMALL"

The "Golden Arches" of Mc Donald's, which had been installed at the first store, were later to be seen by millions of people all over the world. And the French fries, sold by the Mc Donald's that were so outstanding in taste, were also to be eaten by those same people.

Returning to his home in Illinois, Ray set up his first store in Des Plaines. It was here that he was to have to overcome many difficulties before making the store successful. One of the difficulties was ridicule. He was even accused of being crazy. He also had to overcome the difficulty of duplicating the Mc Donald French fry; this alone took three month! Finally the store started to show a profit and Ray was by this time paying attention to the potential of opening three more store in California and eight more were opened in 1956.

When Harry Sonneborn, an expert in finance, joined force with Ray Kroc, things really began to move. Their association gave birth to the Franchise Realty Corporation, which was later to vault the Mc Donald chain to unprecedented success. In 1957, twenty-five more stores were opened.

Always a perfectionist, Ray Kroc viewed executive ability as measured by the fewest mistakes. He also knew that to hire a man to do a job meant to get out of the way and let him do it. Fred Turner now joined the Kroc team and was destined to head up operations. "Quality Service, Cleanliness and value (QSV&C) had become one of the success formulas of the Mc Donald stores and it was to multiple itself many times over.

Dealing with everything from wasted seconds in handling hamburger buns, the proper amount of hamburger patties to be in one stack, more efficient system of receiving deliveries, eventual personality clashes, mechanics liens, financing problems, a costly divorce and other difficulties, Ray Kroc moved on. Although the Mc Donald's stores at last count had passed four thousand, Ray still a dreamer, is looking towards a figure of ten thousand stores. Mc Donald's has also passed the one billion dollar gross income mark.

Ray Kroc, viewing his success as his tribute to free enterprise, went on to save a baseball team for the city of San Diego. This he did through the purchase of the padres when he was in his early 70's yet, he still considers himself as "green and growing"!

Although there have been changes in personnel, changes in store architecture, and additions to the Mc Donald menu, the essential principles of Mc Donald operations are mostly the same. When fighting competition he stresses strength and using one's mind to always stay in front. Always a salesman and promoter, Ray still believes that "There's almost nothing you can't accomplish if you set your mind to it". Work is still his play.

"I'M CONVINCED THAT I'M A WINNER"

SOICHIRO HONDA
* Honda Motor *

Soichiro Honda was born in 1906 in a small village in Japan. Even when he was very young, Motors fascinated him. In fact, it is rare that someone's true calling manifest itself so early in life. In his memoirs, Honda states that, even at the age of two or three, he was vividly Impressed by the sight, but especially the sound of a rice-husking machine on a neighborhood farm.

Honda was a poor student at school. Thanks to a devious stratagem he concocted, he always managed to grab a seat out of the teachers range of vision. Here he was able to daydream or cook up ingenious inventions. "I got poor grades in school. It didn't upset me very much. My universe revolved elsewhere, around engines, motors and bicycles.

"Several years later I learned that the miracle laid in my willpower and repeated attempts. Believing deeply in something allows all of us to find tremendous inner strength and to surpass our limitations." An illustrious character was going to greatly inspire and influence Honda: Napoleon. He learned about him from his father, but didn't know any details of his life.

"I pictured him as a man whose physical size and strength equaled his power and fame. When I found out later in history books that he was short and squat, I wasn't disappointed. I'm not very tall myself and obviously believed that a man shouldn't be measured by his height, but by his actions and the imprint he leaves on the history of mankind. I also learned that napoleon came from a humble background and that his family was probably quite poor. I concluded that it wasn't necessary to be born rich or noble to succeed in life. Other qualities also entitle you to success: courage, perseverance and ambitions".

"What I retained most from this man was the moral or philosophical lesson that guided his future tendencies: a poor young student manages to tomb nose at kings, to clamor for revolution and to dominate the entire western world and one day I too would become a Napoleon short and famous. My dream was to become the Napoleon of mechanics! Napoleon, my dear Napoleon, my childhood idol because both of us were entitled to keep our crazy dreams."

Not much of an intellectual by nature, Honda restricted his reading to a technical magazine called "The world of wheels". One day while leafing through it, he saw an advertisement seeking to hire a garage apprentice for the hart Shokai Company in Tokyo. He applied for the job. A few days latter, he got a positive response. His father begrudgingly allowed him to quit school and head for Tokyo. He was fifteen years old. The job he was given did not quite live up to his ambitious expectations. Instead of being a garage apprentice, he was assigned to baby-sit the boss's youngest child. To all intents and purpose, he was much too young to be given a motor to repair on his own.

"How humiliating! I was so close to my goal, but unable to reach it. Nevertheless this experience strengthened my determination. It would have been downright stupid to drop the kid there and go home defeated, destroying my chances of becoming a mechanic. It is said that every man bears a tiny trace of God's brain. I believe I owe it to the bit I got that I found the patience to stay in Tokyo, to bide my time, and to grab the next opportunity that came my way."

Business was booming; so Mr. Saka Kibara, his boss. Finally decided that it was perhaps time to give this young man a chance. He spent six years learning his trade. "I finally became an independent adult, a real man, the master of my arms, legs, brain, destiny, timetable and the risk facing me". This tremendous sense of freedom is experienced only by those starting up their own businesses. A study carried out as shown that this feeling largely compensate for the anxiety that comes from burning your bridges. However, it appears necessary to have a special kind of character ready to take the plunge' without being paralyzed by material insecurity at the beginning.

His boss, foreseeing a brilliant career ahead of him, was proposing that he starts up a branch in his town. During Honda's long years away from home, many things had changed. For one thing, two or three garage had opened up. Honda thought at first that his would be the only one in town. Now he would some how have to find a way to deal with his competitors and to do more and better than they. He soon discover that he had two ways of doing this: first of all, he would have to accept tricky repair jobs that discouraged the other mechanics and secondly, he would have to work as fast as possible so owners wouldn't be deprived of their vehicles for too long. Honda quickly carved out a solid reputation for him self. Of course he some times had to work all night long to return his customers' cars the following day, but that was the price he was willing to pay. His creative ingenuity became evident then. Back then the spokes in car wheels were made of wood and were not very shock-absorbent. Honda had the idea of replacing them with metal.

When he was thirty years old, Honda signed his first patent. His metal spokes were an instant hit and were exported all over the world. "This invention had opened my eyes to the patience needed to operate in our cottage—like industry. A garage or store is run like a train. It stops at every village and picks up locals, but is unable to go greater distances. Sure, you can be happy chugging up and down this milk—run, but as for myself, I dreamed of operating bigger, faster trains.

He invested all of his savings in 'Tokai Seiki; a piston ring production factory. His first tests were not very successful. The first rings he manufactured were not flexible enough and were simply not marketable. Honda remembers his friends' reactions regarding his failure:

"My friends came in great numbers to tell me that I should have stayed in my garage, expanded it gradually and let my business prosper instead of jumping into shaky ventures. I had invested all of my savings in this scheme. I felt responsible for those I had dragged into this affair and told myself that I was thirty years old and had possible destroyed all of my chances by selling of my garage".

Crushed by the weight of his failure and responsibility, Honda became seriously ill. But, after convalescing for two months, he came back to head his operation, determined to overcome his problems. The local foundries obviously refused to disclose their secrets. He was on his own. He worked day and night to find the solution, but could see none. The pistons he made were always as hard as rock. Even with all the determination in the world, Honda was forced to face facts: he lacked the technical know—how to go any further.

Needless to say, many others in his shoes would have given up at this point, but Honda, swallowing his pride, agreed to go back to school. He enrolled in university courses to complete his engineering training.

Every morning he would go to university and as soon as classes were over would race to his workshop and try to put what he had learned into practices. He stayed there for two years and was finally thrown out. The problem was that Honda, as stubborn as ever, skipped all of his classes except those dealing with manufacturing parts. "I was like a person dying of hunger receiving a long, drawn—out explanation of the general laws of dietetics and their effects instead of being given something to eat".

Honda tried in vain to explain to the director that he wasn't attending school for a diploma but for knowledge. This was a slap in the director's face!

Honda returned to his factory armed with new facts, and began producing better pistons. He had won. Tokai Seiki gradually strengthened its market position and began enjoying a reputation for excellence. The Second World War abruptly put a stop to all this. In June 1945, American bombs destroyed his factories.

After the war ended, Honda decided to take a year off to develop several inventions and to do some thinking. Still optimistic, despite the gloominess that had settled over the country, he set up his own technical research laboratory, firmly intending to safeguard his independence. He had an idea at the back of his mind. The country's economic situation appeared desperate in the eyes of most industrialists. But Honda's diagnosis was just the opposite.

Spurred on by the rebirth of his business, Honda opened a motorcycle assemble plant on February 1948. But he couldn't stop there—he had to do better. On September 24, 1948, Honda set up the Honda Motor Company. But until in August 1949, that the first prototype was born. It was called 'dream' the new motor had a capacity of only 98cc and 3 horsepower. Despite Honda's first success, he now faced heavy financial problems.

One of his old friends introduced him to Takeo Fujisawa, a gifted administrator, who helped save Honda's budding company. This association between the two, one a dreamer, the other a manager, is a good example of the principle that nobody forges his success completely on his own. Referring to the human factor, Honda says: "When I take temporary stock of my life, I measure how important contacts are, how this is worth more than all machine inventions because meeting people allows us to expand our vision of things and get thousands of different experiences that we would never have had otherwise".

Far from letting 'Dream' discourage him almost 10 years later this same model would be copied by producer's world wide. Honda said: "I never basically regretted the public's first reactions. They forced me to push my talents to the limit and create a motor that was way ahead of its time". Honda was then faced with the need to increase production, modernize his factory and even set up new plants. To do this, his needed capital and lots of it. For someone not part of the establishment, a self-made man in the full sense of the word, convincing the bank to lend him the necessary money was not going to be easy! But Honda was very persuasive and the banks agreed. He modernized his plant and started manufacturing 25,000 bikes a month, sold in 13,000 Honda distributorships. The five factories he owned made him a millionaire.

Honda went to Europe and bought the best bikes on the market. He brought them home, took them apart, studied them carefully and created his own racing bikes. They were then entered in races and were highly successful. Honda subsidiaries sprang up in countries across the world, including the United State, Germany, France, England, Switzerland, Belgium, Australia, Canada, Brazil, Mexico, Peru and Thailand.

What he had accomplished with motorcycles, he now hoped to do with cars. In 1962, the Honda Motor Company officially declared that it was entering the field of car manufacturing. Honda did not have an easy task, because it meant that he was now facing competition from the United State, which dominated the world market.

Once again; Honda chose to rely on competition to pierce this market and so he entered his cars in the prestigious formula one races. Despite the problems he at first encountered, Honda's dream came true on October 24, 1965. one of his entries came first in a major competition, beating world—famous cars such as Ferrari and Lotus the products of firms who had years of experience in racing and research. Encouraged by these wins, Honda decided to produce cars for the general public in 1967 and again trying to produce low—consumption vehicles, he decided to stick to small cars. That was a right move.

Honda's outstanding success story is especially enlightening since it illustrates the principle that it is possible to succeed not only when starting from scratch, but under very difficult circumstances as well. During six post-war periods, Japan lay in ruins. The average salary was about six hundred pounds starlings a year. The so called Japanese miracle is undoubtedly due to individual such as Honda. Remember his example when you complain that the economic situation is preventing you from growing rich.

Over the years, Honda took care to write down in his memoirs the major principles of his success. To conclude his story, here is his recipe for success summed up in five points:

- Always be ambitious and youthful

- Respect sound theories, find new ideas and devote time to improving production

- Take pleasure in your work and try to make working conditions as pleasant as possible

- Constantly look for a smooth, harmonious working rhythm

- Always keep in mind the value of research and hard work.

DORATHY WALTERS
* Dottie Walters *

One night in 1948, Dorathy Walter's, husband came home from his dry cleaning establishment, sad and crushed. His business was on the verge of collapsing and everything they had worked for could be wiped out. Dottie asked Bob only one question; "Bob, can you hold on for one more month?" He said he would try.

Turning to the Bible, Dottie read the tale of the widow, who, despairing of losing her two sons into slavery, asked Elisha, "what can I do"? This sage answered: "what has thou in thy house"? The widow only had a little oil, but she greatly prospered by selling it to her friends and neighbors. She then turned to the story of the talents. What talent did she possess?

In 1948 Dottie Walters was a very young house wife with two little babies. What treasure had she that people would purchase? How could she multiply her "talent" in this time of financial crises? The Bible words, "for unto every one that hath shall be given, and he shall have abundance," gave her a new vision of what she must do.

In high school Dottie had written a column for the school paper, she decided on a course of action. "This is my one talent," she declared the next day she pushed her two babies down town in a Taylor Tot to a weekly news-paper office. She talked a hard-nosed publisher into selling her advertising column on credit.

Then, with her babies still in tow, Dottie called on local merchants in hopes of selling them ad space. She was shy and more than a little scared, but she persisted. Her "talent" began multiplying, until her sponsors—a garage man—told her, "Why don't you start a hospitality hostess service"?

Dottie thought over and decided why not give it a go. She purchased a model A Ford for fifty dollars. She decorated a large basket with flowers and bows. Inside there were such items as food, candy, maps of the town, coupon booklets and other literatures. She then would Proceed with her two children with her, to the address of new arrivals in Baldwin Park, California. "Good morning, my name is Dottie Walters. I'm here to welcome you to Baldwin Park".

Soon Dottie was making 100 or more calls monthly. Each merchant who subscribed to her service paid to fixed amount for each call she made. In time she had to hire other women to help her with her rapidly expanding business. Husband Bob soon sold his dry cleaning business and joined Dottie in her growing venture.

Dottie Walter's Hospital Hostess Service today welcomes five thousand new residents to southern California each month. She services an area known as the "Golden Triangle"—from Los Angels to San Diego.

Dorothy has also authored several books on success and motivations sub-jects, including the best-selling "the selling power of a women" (published by Frederick Fell). She also has become one of the most sought after women speakers in the world. A member and former officer of the National Speakers Association, Dottie has spoken at motivational rallies worldwide, often shar-ing the platform with the most famous speakers in the world (Norman Vin-cent Peal, Art Link-letter, etc). She also publishes a lively newsletter for public speakers, and those who wish to become speakers, called "sharing ideas among professional speakers".

Dorothy Walter is a positive proof of what any woman (or man) can do with the help of faith desire and determination.

CONRAD NICHOLSON HILTON
* Hilton Hotels *

Hilton was born on Christmas Day 1887 in San Antonio, New Mexico. He was the second of eight children and the first son. Conrad and his brothers and sisters mastered Spanish at an early age, since they were growing up among Mexican Immigrants. As his father was much too busy to help raise his large family, Hilton was most influenced by his mother. She was the one who instilled in him faith, respect for honesty and love of truth, value that would guide him throughout his life. He once admitted that he delighted in the company of frank men and was instinctively horrified by dishonesty, adding that he could not conceive of ever rejoicing for one moment in having earned a single dollar through cupidity or trickery.

Since Hilton had seemed much more interested in business than in religion, his mother began to worry a little about him. During his summer vacation, Hilton worked in his father's shop. His father paid him five dollar a month, which was generous sum back then. His father told him that if he showed more interest in the business, he would double his salary. By accepting his father's offer, Hilton was subconsciously obeying the golden rule of hard work; the basis for fortunes built the world over. His father was thrilled at Conrad passion for business. Connie, as he was called, ingeniously contrived to increase his income by selling the vegetables he grew himself in his own garden. His success earned him family's admiration. That summer, Hilton managed to earn fifty dollar. His father was always eager for school holidays to begin because he recognized that Conrad was gifted with a rare business talent and would probably carve out an extraordinary place for himself in the future.

Hilton was now studying at the Mexico Military Institute, but his business successes made him think about leaving school His dad understood his son's passion for business and urged him in this direction by raising his salary to twenty—five dollars a month. This was in 1904 and business was booming for the Hilton family by now quite comfortable indeed. His father had earned one hundred and thirty five thousand dollars by selling a coal mine he had bought several years earlier at an incredibly low price. To celebrate this event, he took his family on a luxury holiday to Chicago. This vacation was a turning point for Connie. For the rest of his life he would always have a preference for first class travel, good hotels and fast cars.

The family's happiness did not last long, however, Hilton's mother became seriously ill. His dad decided to move to long Beach California. Then disaster struck—the economic crisis of 1907. Prices plummeted and his dad rapidly lost his money. Of course the shop was stocked with orders he had just filled at low cost, but prices had fallen lower than that and money was so short that all his sales were carried out at a loss.

He came up with an idea of going into the hotel business. The dad had explained to his family that they were bankrupt, but that this had happened before and was nothing to be afraid of. He reminded them that their mother was in good health again and that this was the most important thing of all. But they had to survive some how, and he wondered if they had any ideas.

Hilton's career was launched as he replied calmly:

"Why not use five or six of the rooms in our house and turn them into bedrooms, like hotel. This town needs a hotel. We might not have clients at the beginning but the news will travel and then it'll run on its own steam. The girls and mother can take care of the kitchen and I'll look after the luggage. We can easily put up several guests in each room. At two dollars fifty cent a day. I think we can manage quite well".

Clearly the major problem was to attract clients. This marked the start of a period of extremely hard work for Hilton. His mother and sisters took care of the hotel itself while he and his father continued working in the store. But as soon as the store closed at 6.pm, Hilton had a light supper and went straight to bed. At midnight he would get up to meet the people getting off the 1 a.m train. He saw to their luggage, got them registered, checked to see whether they had everything they needed, such as blankets, soap and towels, jotted down what they wanted for breakfast in the morning and at what time they wished to be woken up. He then posted these notes up for his mother and sisters to see and returned to the train station to do the same thing over again for the 3.am train. When the last traveled had settled in for the night, Hilton could finally get some sleep, at least until 7. am, when he would get up, take care of the guests and then open the store up at 8.am.

It took only six weeks for the news to spread throughout the area and even as Far East as Chicago. "if you're forced to make a stopover, people would say, 'make sure you do it in San Antonio and get a room at the Hiltons'". The lesson Conrad Hilton learned was an important one. He was always willing to work long and hard to succeed. Until his death, he would say that he wouldn't take a million dollars in exchange for all the things he learned during this time. Hilton learned an invaluable lesson: "if you work with steadfast determination long enough, you will make your dream come true".

Again Hilton dreamed of opening a chain of banks. To put his hands on the capital he needed, he went to Texas, where oil was helping to build many entrepreneurs' fortunes. He was unable to buy a bank in San Francisco, but happened to spot the bustling Mobley Hotel. From then on, he was to be a hotel man.

He bought the Mobley Hotel for forty thousand dollars. During the next few months he worked non-stop. He slept on a sofa in his office, since all the rooms were occupied. This is where he learned a rule that would serve him well throughout his career and would generate his colossal fortune. Not a single square inch must be wasted in a hotel. He also discovered his famous principle, which he called 'Minimax'. "Minimum price, Maximum service".

He began to make radical changes in the hotel. Since the restaurant was not generating any profits, he converted it into bedroom space. The reception desk was cut down to half it's size to open up a little boutique.

Three sofas and a canopy were removed from the foyer to make room for a stall. When he redesigned the first floor of the New York Plaza Hotel he included the 'Oak Room Bar', which increased the profit from this floor from five thousand dollars to over twenty thousand dollars a year.

Hilton believed that any businessman who wanted to succeed would have to apply the following rule religiously: "Abhor wasted space, wasted efforts and wasted money in other words convert everything into gold and constantly search for that gold mine". For Hilton, it was essential for each of his hotels to have it's own personality. "I buy tradition and do every thing to get the maximum benefit from it".

During his rise in the hotel business, several shrewd businessmen backed Hilton. In 1946, the Hilton Hotel Corporation was founded with Hilton named as chairman. His company reached its peak when on October 12, 1949, Hilton announced that he had just purchased the Waldorf—Astoria Hotel, with its 1,900 rooms, this hotel was the most luxuries of American hotels then. This was a moment Conrad Hilton had been dreaming of for years. At this time he had become a sharp minded negotiator. Negotiations had lasted several months. His associate and advisers came out of these meetings completely worn out. Beside the meetings, they had to continue doing their normal day—to—day work. Hilton also made sure that they all got up at 6.15 a.m and led them to church for a half hour prayers. They all obediently followed him, even those who were not Catholics. One of his associate later said: "when Conrad prays for something, he gets it, perhaps because he never forgets to give thanks to the one he prayed to".

When the wheeling and dealings for the Waldorf—Astoria finally came to an end his partner crawled into bed figuring that they could at least sleep in the next day. This was underestimating Hilton! At 6.15 the next morning, their phones rang as usual. When they were all assembled, one of them grumbled: "why go back church now that the waldorf is ours for good". Hilton tartly replied: "you can't pray for something you want and forget to give thanks when you get it lets go!"

There was still one area, which appealed to Hilton's spirit of adventure the overseas market. He applied the same principles there as those that had made him one of the richest men in America. This rule was useful when he made his first oversees purchase, "show due respect towards whoever you are dealing with". This principle helped him in his dealings with the Puerto Rican government, who had approached seven American hotels to open up a luxury hotel in San Juan. None of them were interested and replied with a curt business letter in English. Hilton wrote his inperfect Spanish. Naturally this struck the right note and the caribe—Hilton hotel chain was born.

In his business deals abroad like at home, Hilton also relied on three rules:

1. Invest your own capital
2. Treat bankers like friends

3.   Give your managers a share in the firm.

This formula met with success wherever he went. Since it avoided ruffling the feathers of the people he dealt with overseas. Hilton preferred offering foreign investors a partnership in his hotel. They bought the land and paid the construction costs. Hilton provided technical assistance and helped put the hotel into operation. The both parties signed a general lease or a general management contract. The personnel, carefully screened and selected on site were invited to perfect their skills in Hilton Hotels in the United States.

Foreign hotels were beginning to spring up everywhere, so Hilton International Corporation was set—up in 1948. This company was independent of the parent company, but Hilton was its president and chairman. Hilton's overseas operations represented two of his ideal: first of all, it would help Americans get acquainted with the rest of the world, which would promote greater tolerance and secondly, these hotels would allow the world to discover America and its citizens.

Well—known personalities helped finance Hilton Hotels abroad. The shah of Iran was the owner of a Hilton through the Pahlari foundation. Howard Hughes was also associated with it through Trans World Airlines. In May 1967, Hilton International became a subsidiary of TWA. Hilton, by then, had retired from the business he had built up from scratch. Hilton finally had the time to enjoy his family and friends in his mansion in California.

A man who revolutionized the hotel industry and became one of the greatest hotel magnates in the world. Hilton headed 185 hotels in the United States and 75 overseas when he died at the age of 91 in January 1979.

In the preface to the biography by Whitney Bolton, Conrad Hilton declared:
"it is impossible for a man to start out in life without knowing which direction he wants to go in. As far as I can remember. I have been branded with the mark of enthusiasm. With enthusiasm to propel me and prayer to shield me, I can say that I like what I have done with my life. Inevitably, with such assets, it would be difficult not to lead a life that is active, rich and above all, happy give a man ambition to spur him, faith to guide him, and good health to allow

him to realize his full potentials and he inevitably has to reach success in one way or the other".

Obviously the success Hilton mentioned here began very early in life. His rise to fame and fortune was due not to the administrative talent needed to run a luxury hotel, but to his business acumen. He mastered the art of finance and became an excellent negotiator, extraordinarily prudent in all his transactions. Furthermore, he had a highly refined sixth sense, which gave him a perfect sense of timing, and he also had a keen eye for recognizing good investment opportunities. Besides, Hilton respected this fundamental law: "choose competent people, place them in key positions and trust their judgment implicitly".

Skills are acquired. At the start of Hiltons life in the real world, when his father gave him the option of staying in San Antonio and taking care of the store, while the rest of the family would move to Sirocco where he had just bought land to build a house. Hilton hated that town and knew that his sister would stand a better chance there, so he agreed, to stay back. This was according to him, the beginning of his apprenticeship in the world of business. He later said that this period taught him everything he needed to know: "to do business honesty to rely on common sense and above all never to be afraid of being bold when necessary".

"I LEARNED THAT YOU WILL NEVER GET ANYWHERE IF YOU PARK YOURSELF COMFORTABLE IN AN EASY CHAIR"

Hilton's life was not a case of one success story after another. Earlier on before his breakthrough in the hotel business, once an old prospector had tempted him with promises of huge profits to be made from silver mine he had discovered. Hilton financed the affair, bought a license and left with the prospector. Unfortunately, the man died soon after and Hilton lost his investment. Also successful in business as it were, Hilton was less happy in his private life. He and his first wife, Mary Barron, had three sons, Nick, Barron and Eric. When the youngest was born in 1933 Hilton was harried, exhausted and crushed under the weight of the hard work he was putting in. His marriage fell apart. He later married Zsa Zsa Gabor, but this lasted only briefly. His third marriage was much less turbulent, in 1976; at the age of 89 he married Mary Frances Kelly. She was 20 years younger and a long—time friend of his.

This man of vision imposed his mark on the world—that is what we call 'making maximum impact'. In 1965, the company formed by Hilton owned 61 hotels in 19 countries; in other words, it had 40,000 rooms and 400,000 employees. of course you know that today these figures have quadrupled by much. Hilton personally controlled thirty percent of the enormous revenues estimated at over billions of dollars.

This is a clear illustration of the principle

"HAVE FAITH IN YOUR IDEA, YOUR DESTINY AND IN GOD"

This formula sums up the phenomenal career of Conrad Nicholson Hilton one of the greatest and richest hotel magnates in the world.

"ALL HARDWORK BRINGS PROFIT, BUT MERE TALKS LEAD ONLY TO POVERTY"

—Proverbs 14:23.

CONTANCE BOUCHER
* Determined productions *

Determined productions became the name of the company that vaulted Constance Boucher to the status of millionaires. Today her creations and promotions are sold in many parts of the world. Connie Boucher has been interested in business since childhood. Always making and building something, one of the first earning ventures was fixing hair for women in her neighborhood.

Connie learned the art of sales woman ship when she was a high school student. Working in many sections of a department store, she sold everything from needles to gloves. She displayed an enthusiasm that was contiguous and, in most cases, she out—sold her co-workers.

Always of a creative nature, Connie later obtained work in interior design shops and did window displays for department stores. She had taken art classes in school and grew to consider her work as fun. Designing a window display for one of the Joseph Magnin stores, Connie got the idea for her first business venture. She was doing charitable work, at the same time, to help raise fund for the children's Home society. The charity group had decided to use Noah's Ark as the theme for their promotion activities. Connie was even successful at selling the Coast Guard on hauling an old barge from another city; she wanted to make everything as realistic as possible. She had also designed a Noah's Ark coloring book for children as a means for raising additional fund for the children's Home. Getting Magnins and other stores to sell the coloring book to help out with the charity drive, Connie began to notice the popularity of the book. It was then that she recognized the business potential.

"Winnie—the—pooh" had been one of Connie's favorite literary experiences as a child. The "pooh" illustrations, she decided, would make excellent materials for the next coloring book. James Young, another Magnin employee joined her effort and suggested that the next book be increased to a larger than usual size. After buying the right for five hundred dollars to use "Winnie—the—pooh" illustrations, a 15" x 18" "pooh" coloring book was published. Connie and her husband had obtained funds for publishing by mortgaging their homes. Yet she had not even sold her first order when the book went into production.

Her husband had suggested to he that the only thing she had going for herself was determination; this was the foundation of what was to become her new company—Determined Productions, Incorporated. Connie was a believer in the idea that if one wanted to do something badly enough, the best thing was to just go ahead and do it; although she was only able to place about six books in each of the first stores she contacted, the books were quickly sold out and she received orders for more. Within six months 52,000 copies were sold, netting forty thousand dollars to the fledgling determined productions.

More coloring books followed; "the wind in the willows", "Alice in wonderland" and "the wizard of OZ". Looking for avenues of growth, Connie expanded her promotions to other cities by contacting people who were advertised distributors. Two of the distributors were high power sales women and orders from distant cities flowed in.

Connie obtained promotions through life and look magazines by getting them to do stories on what she called "pooh parties". "Pooh" characters and fixtures were created on a tract of land, children were invited and life magazine provided three page coverage on the activities.

Although there were a few "character" products on the market at the time (the 1960s), the range was limited. On a visit to Europe, cannie had noticed that the novelty—gift business was more active than in America. Sensing that the novelty—gift business in America was due for considerable growth, she decided to go after the characters in the "peanuts" Comie strip. Her thinking on both issues was soon to be proven correct.

With James Young as full time art director, Connie and determined productions began to rollout "peanuts" products. "Snoopy" stuffed animals; cloths and toys were sold everywhere. Watches sleeping bags and shirts bearing the "snoop" emblem became commonplace. Even the Japanese became 'snoopy-ized'. Determined productions reaped millions from the venture, an it was only the beginning.

A royalty arrangement had been worked out with United Features Syndicate, the owners of the right, to use the characters of Charles Schultz Peanuts Comie strip. The agreement provided that determined could contract with other firms to make products with 'peanuts characters on them. J.P Stevens, a linen manufacturer, is reported to have sold Ten million dollars worth of 'peanuts' bedding in one year" a record for any single pattern sale.

Now located in San Francisco, California, determined Production has branched out into other lines. A restaurant, television and motion pictures are being considered. Offices and syndications have been established as far Tokyo, Switzerland and Hong Kong.

A closely held corporation, determined productions do not release sales figures. However, it has been reported (by an independent financial service) that determined productions volume has now reached twenty million dollars in annual sales. Constant Boucher, energetic, organized full of new ideas and now millionaires, says that she will not quit "until I can't navigate".

JOHN DAVISON ROCKEFELLER
* Standard Oil *

The man the multimillionaire steel king, Andrew Carnegie first nicknamed 'Reckafellow' and then later 'my co-millionaire' was born in 1839 in a small farmhouse near Moravia in the state of New York.

As a child he earned pocket money be selling small painted rocks to his friends. Instead of spending the pennies he made he accumulated them in a blue earthenware bowl stashed away at the top of a chest of drawers in the family sitting room. According to him, it was his first strong box. As a result of these financial operations, he had soon saved fifty dollars.

These fifty dollars were going to determine the boy's future. A neighboring farmer needed this amount to settle an urgent debt; John Rockefeller willingly lent it to him, but charges him seven percent interest! The farmer agreed. One year later, Rockefeller received three dollars fifty cent in interest besides the capital he had lent out. He would later write that from that day on I was determined to make money work for me." He had just learned that money makes money.

Hence forth, all of his profits were carefully registered in a small book, which he called 'ledger A'. Some people even said that towards the end of his life John Rockefeller still kept the book containing the treasures of his youth. Ledger A is, to some extent, Rockefeller's autobiography, since in his eyes the figure listed there were more eloquent than words. He declared: learn to make figures talk! They will tell you harsh truth and will reveal the future.

When he graduated from school in 1855 Rockefeller decided to enter the world that fascinated him so much. I tried the railroads, banks, and wholesalers, ignoring all insignificant establishments. I was looking for an important enterprise!"

On September 26,1855,he got his first job at Hewitt & Tuttle, a brokerage company handling grain and vegetables. This was a decisive moment in his life. Every year until his death in 1937, a flag was raised on the mast towering over his estate, pocantico, on the shores of the Hudson River, to commemorate this anniversary.

He began work at 6:30 a.m every morning. He was so efficient that his bosses congratulated themselves for having appointed such a talented employee. John Rockefeller made business his religion. In bed at night, he would mull over the days financial operations, trying to discover how he could have made them more profitable!

He always told himself: "This is a good opportunity. But be careful. False pride is a trap: Don't be hasty, don't make blunders. Your future depends on every passing day." Henceforth his philosophy would be: "Discipline, order, and a faithful account of all debits and credits."

In 1858 he was earning six—hundred dollars a year, but, aware of his value to the firm, he asked for a two—thousand dollars raise. His bosses refused. It was then that he decided to set up his own company with an acquaintance of his, Maurice Clark, an Englishman 12 years his senior who was working for a brokerage house. Rockefeller had saved Eight—hundred dollars, but needed one—thousand dollars to start up his commission and forwarding business. He determined to ask his father for a loan. His father agreed, but charged 10 percent interest every year until he had paid off the loan. He was then 18 years old!

At the beginning of his career, Rockefeller was often forced to rely on his father, and each time had to pay the same yearly interest rate. About this he latter wrote: "This discipline should have done me some good. Perhaps it did, but in truth, although I carefully hide it from him, I did not really appreciate my father's policy of pulling a fast one on me just to see if my financial acumen was equal to his tricks." Clark and Rockefeller's company made four—thousand dollars in profits during the first year. The second year was even more profitable, and the profits rose to seventeen—thousand dollars.

In 1861, the civil war broke out. Although a source of misery for the vast majority of people, it was the key to their fortune! It was all a matter of organization, method, attention to detail, and ruthless contracts all areas in which Rockefeller excelled. From that time on, their success was guaranteed.

Rockefeller brought to his business an inborn seriousness of purpose. He was pious until the day he died and regularly went to a small Baptist church in Cleveland while he lived there. In fact, he always gave part of his profits to the church, even when he was a multi-millionaire.

At this time a revolution was taking place. In 1859, two years before the American Civil War, Edwin Drake had struck oil in Titusville, Pennsylvania. Until then oil had been viewed only as a source of medication and as lighting fuel. Drake's discovery sparked a great oil rush. For many in business, it was a unique investment opportunity, but it didn't impress Rockefeller. Astute as ever, he realized that if there was any money to be made it would be in transportation and refining, not in drilling. Since the transport system was in chaos and refining methods practically non existent, John Rockefeller chose to wait for a better time.

Four year later, the Atlantic and West Railroad Company built a new line to Cleveland, joining it with New York and passing right through the oil region. The time was now ripe! At this time, Rockefeller had met Samuel Andrews, one of Clark's acquaintances, at the Baptist church. It didn't take Clark and Andrew long to infect Rockefeller with their enthusiasm for black gold. Rockefeller, who was still only 23 years old, invested four thousand dollars in the new Clark, Andrew and company.

He duly noted the following in his ledger: "at 2.p.m, married Miss L.C. Spellman, celebrated by the reverend D. Wolcott, assisted by Reverend Paige in the young girl's home". Once married, he went back to his business affairs. Refineries were mushrooming in Cleveland, which was becoming one of the most important oil centres. Rockefeller slowly began to show more interest in the oil business, abandoning the grain commissioning business. His strict discipline brought him commercial dividends. In a town full of wily dealers he was considered to be one of the shrewdest, best informed traders.

For one who had been so reluctant at first, Rockefeller was now the most enthusiastic of all the partners. Even with assets of one hundred thousand dollars, Clark was afraid of the expansion recommended by Rockefeller, who believed that: "The golden rule of success is expansion". Clark obstinately refused to follow this course. They had reached an impasse. There was one solution and that was to auction the company. This took place on February 2, 1865. the bidding rose until clerk stopped at seventy-two thousand dollars. Rockefeller snapped: seventy-two thousand five-hundred dollars. Clark, defeated, said: "All right, John it's yours'.

The company, now called Rockefeller and Andrews became the largest refinery in Cleveland, with a capacity of 500 barrels a day and annual revenue of one million dollars. Rockefeller's mind was totally free of doubt; he had absolute faith in the future. He was going to bend fate to his will!

He also knew how to attract valuable employees, such as Henry M. Flagler, who had won and lost fortunes, but was now rich again after a profitable marriage. He was only one of the many bold directors Rockefeller placed at the helm of his company. "The ability to handle people is a commodity that can be bought like sugar and coffee and I'm willing to pay more for it than for any other commodity in the world".

What he meant was that success was built on several ingredients and one of the most important is knowing how to choose associates who are honest, loyal, and totally devoted to the leaders ideals. Rockefeller, with his proverbial mania for detail, was supremely successful in this.

On January 10, 1870, he founded a new company with a capital stock of one million dollars—'standard oil'. At this time, standard oil was one of the largest oil refineries in this region of the united state. But Rockefeller had the idea of including other smaller refineries in the gigantic business he was creating. So in 1872, he struck a deal with the rail-way companies that help him save one dollar twenty—five cent than the normally two dollar fifty cent cost. That was a preferential rate. It was a stroke of genius. The poorer his competitors got, the richer Rockefeller became. Barely three month later, Rockefeller bought out 22 of the 23 refineries in Cleveland? Standard oil was now refining a quarter of all American oil!

When he had started his company, Rockefeller had 15 competitors in New York, 12 in Philadelphia, 22 in Pittsburg and 27 in the rest of the country. In the end, there was only one oil company—standard oil! In April 1878, Flagler mentioned in a study presented to the Board of Directors, that the total refining Capacity in the United State was 36 million barrels a day. Standard oil alone refined 33 million.

In 1880, 95 percent of the total refining capacity was fulfilled by standard oil. Through sheer obstinacy, discipline, constant work, and unwavering faith in his destiny, Rockefeller had become what he had always wanted to be: 'The Emperor of Capitalism'!

But Rockefeller strength did not lie in innovation (which he distrusted, especially because of its financial implications), but in the organization and deployment of power. His principle was: "Method and Organization".

In 1882, Rockefeller set up a trust. The law forbade companies to do business in state other than their own, so Rockefeller got around this law through his trust. From then on, there would be Standard Oil of New York. Standard Oil of New Jersey, Standard Oil of Pennsylvania and so on.

Rockefeller created one of the most powerful financial empires that had ever existed. The team comprised the most astute financiers in the united state. And all were millionaires! During an inquiry into standard oil's affairs, William Vanderbilt declared to the senate:

"I have never met a group of men as informed and able as they in business. I do not believe it is possible to make them put down their banner by legislative decree or any other way, neither in this state nor any other. Nothing can be done about them. They will always have the upper hand."

By the end of the century, industrial technology had created dozens of oil by—products. Standard's revenues were astronomical! Standard oil seemed to be everywhere. In 1903, standard offered it's gas and lubricating oil to Wright brothers. Shortly afterwards the south improvement company, an organization uniting refiners and railways companies to protect their respective interests, caused a scandal, and Rockefeller became the victim of virulent attacks and slanderous remarks, both in the press and in political circles. He defended himself by saying: "it was my right; my conscience told me it was my right. Every thing was clear between the Lord and myself".

Rockefeller remained silent at the time, but later commented: "look at the earthworm over there on the ground if I step on it, I am attracting attention to it. If I ignore it, it disappears". Unfortunately, far from disappearing, the scandal grew more intense. Rockefeller became, in a sense the symbol of the malaise of those times. He received death threats. When he went to church, people would gather to insult him. The minister of the church had to hire private detectives to circulate among the crowed outside and in the church to watch over Rockefeller. Rockefeller himself always kept a loaded revolver next to his bed.

But nothing could put a halt to standard's expansion; standard oil's best world agents (since the united state had become too small a market for the company) were the members of the American Diplomatic Corps! To detect new markets and outsell its competitors, especially the Russians, whose oil was beginning to sell all over Europe, standard oil gained access to secret reports. These were sent to Rockefeller by ambassadors. Many of them received payment for their 'services' from standard's secret funds.

Rockefeller's personal fortune in 1897 had reached two—hundred million dollars. The irony was that it was during his retirement that he earned most, since the internal combustion engine, marketed in 1913, quadrupled his earnings. From two—hundred million dollars to over.

One—billion dollars. Determined to clear his name and secretly persuaded that his fortune was a gift from God rewarding him for services rendered to humanity, he launched himself into philanthropy!

Rockefeller sincerely believed that God had given him money and that this was the one and only secret of his phenomenal success. To the surprised reporter to whom he had just made this declaration, he explained: "I believed that the power of making money is a gift from God, to be developed and used the best we can for the good of humanity. Having received a share of this gift, I believe it is my duty to make money more and more money and to use this money for the good of my fellow man by listening to the voice of my conscience".

Rockefeller's problem was not over, however. The hatred for this self—made man was astonishing. The Government was bent on dissolving the trust. A detailed study was undertaken and the true extent of Rockefeller's power became known. In 21 volumes, including 14,485 detailed testimonies, it was discovered that the young brokers initial four—thousand dollars investment now produced 35,000 barrels of refined petrol and oil a day and included a pipeline stretching over 150,000km and 100 tankers to transport his products abroad! In fact, the trust was worth six hundred and sixty million dollars!

The government finally brought standard oil to its knees. The company was split up into 39 smaller companies, supposedly independent of one another. But once again, Rockefeller recovered from defeat. However, he converted this 'failure' into a success. The share of the newly founded companies quadrupled and so Rockefeller wealth multiplied three or four times.

From the on, Rockefeller had one preoccupation: 'to give.' And Gates, his new right—hand man, was well suited for this job. In 1901, the Rockefeller Institute for Medical Research was founded, the first of its kind in America. Then in 1903, the General Education Board was created to oversee education for black people. Later, Rockefeller saw to it that this institute served to promote a better national system of higher education. After this came the sanitation commission.

This commission finally brought public opinion back on to Rockefeller's side. The Rockefeller Foundation, incidentally, is still the largest philanthropic organization in the world. Some people claimed that Rockefeller began these charities only after he had made his fortune. Yet his ledger A clearly indicates that he set aside part of his very first earning to give to his church. He continued to do this all his life. In later years his annual donations rose to over one million dollars.

Reconciled with the public, to whom he believed himself responsible Rockefeller retired to his mansion at Pocantico Hills. He called it 'Kikjuit' the Dutch term for 'look—out' and here he could enjoy a well—deserved rest. Despite his old age, he did not lose the sense of humor that most people were unaware of .

During a massage session, upon hearing his bones crack, he said with a touch of irony: They say I control all the oil in the country and I haven't enough even to oil my own joint". To the sculptor making his bust, he asked whether it would be possible to make his sketch while he was playing golf. "I can't carry my clay with me!' he protested. Rockefeller laconically replies: "why not? I carry mine with me all the time!"

He kept an eye on his interest, especially his works of charity, until the last day of his life. Both in this sphere and in business, Rockefeller was able to make good use of his organizational talents, gifts from God which he had managed to make bear fruit beyond his greatest expectations.

John David Rockefeller died in 1937. Faithful to his great principle,

"TIME IS MONEY".

In concluding this chapter let me remind you of this: the next time you drive a Ford, Benz or Honda Car—think creativity—and when next you walk into any Mc Donald's restaurant, Hilton Hotel or buy a bottle of Coca-Cola think Business—that is the power of dreams actualized because of a system called free enterprise or Plain still 'Capitalism'.

8

'LINKING
THE
DOTS'

THE NEW VISIONERS

"In the free market one gains wealth only through serving the consumer best, as determined by the opinion of those very consumer themselves"

—John Hospers

We've heard of the Rockefellers, Carnegies, Hiltons, Hondas, fords, krocs, Candlers, Edisons, Spielberg's, onass is; Trumps, Watsons, etc. Now each one of those people recognized the opportunity for making it big in their various sectors and industries—they capitalized on it to meet a market demand.

All successful businessmen thoroughly understood the needs of the consumer, and knew exactly what they could do to help serve the consumer and create a niche for themselves. This could only be made possible in a de—centralized system of free enterprise. They had the freedom to do so. And every other person also had the freedom to do so. Therefore, in the free enterprise system, people who could best serve the consumers are paid awesomely for their achievements.

Now. Understand this; most of if not all the examples of the successful businessmen and woman we have chronicled their lives contradicts what is commonly said on our streets today. Remember, they first worked as Clerks, mechanics, salesmen etc some started hotel with a five rooms. Owned are kiosks before tuning it to a supermarket and then chains of supermarkets. They failed in one area before entering into another, so on. This completely contrary to the common people believe that the time of opportunity is over, or even more commonly that those opportunities do not exist for Africa. The places of becoming a millionaire is restricted into some few hot spots there is no way a Carnegie or a Rockefeller could have made it in Africa especially in these our time, it is much more difficult to make a million naira now than it were those days.

Listen to me friends the days of opportunities in Africa has just arrived. The only problems that exist is the barriers we have created inside our minds. Those negative thoughts, believes and confessions are not doing us any good.

Yes financial fortune has been made in those places we tag as conducive, but fortune is being built also in Africa right now. Greater fortunes will be made in the future right here in Africa. New individuals with great visions and quality perspective are already rising from this continent. They are solving the economic problem of Africa and also riding in financial majesty in the flux of changing global condition.

The presence of economic depression being felt now in the continent will in no where impede the creation of new industrial giants and captains of business, or even the growth of new enterprises.

Africa is still a place we can be proud of. Even if we are not, we don't have no place to call our own. But truth is our potentials are envied by our friends and foes alike.

The civilized world know that majority of the resources use to develop their regions is coming out of Africa. They also know that the future of industrial revolution belongs to Africa. They have also realized the fact that African are fast emancipating their minds as to their benefit of the free Market and learning very quickly the logics of good business principle and all its potentials to change their lives. Africa, no doubt is fast becoming the envy of the civilized world. Truth is, the time for African to reign as a king has finally arrived. Wake up all you inhabitant of this land, sound the trumpet loud that every African can run with this message—"Africa is redeemed". We will not die in poverty and war, but we will live to proclaim the mighty works that God has placed in our hands.

Visioners are coming out of Africa than never before. It doesn't take much to see how enormously different our lives have developed compared to some years ago when we are only worthless slaves. Satellites are being launched by Africa countries, well designed cars, Television and radio sets and several modern technological equipment are now being manufactured in Africa. Giant pharmaceutical companies are springing up, Telecommunication is taking a whole new dimension and the future of energy solidly belongs to Africa. More still, more and more people are beginning to enjoy true democracy as a system of governance.

Just some couple of years ago we were slaves working in vast plantation farms, then slaves working in our own countries under colonial regimes. In those times, we covered long distances on bear foots and couldn't read or write. Now not only can we read or write we do speak so many foreign languages.

People are too amazed as to the inventions coming out of Africa, the rate of growth of its citizens, the amount of her resources and potentials and the way we have embraced democracy.

Wherever man has been free to think, societal has been blessed with a few productive visioners and patriarchs who step to the frontline every day and in everyway bringing out brilliant creative ideas and capitalizing on their potentials to meet a market demand. They are giving birth to new companies. This new visioners with great ideas, who have the courage and strength to use that idea and meet a market need of the consuming public can't but take a share of the market itself.

Visioners of course eventually get tired, old and they die but not without passing on the mantle of their enterprise unto people who in most cases may be less competent than themselves. Now this provide the opportunity for a more effective and efficient individual to also as well cut away a share of the market themselves. Consumers always want the best product and a better rate. The producer who best fits into the consumers wants will be the one they'll patronize—no matter how small or big, new or old such may be.

The whole idea of the free enterprise/free market system is geared toward satisfying the consumer with the product or service they want. Those enterprise who are successful at satisfying the consumers are richly rewarded through much sales. So the competition ensures that the one, who best satisfy those needs, gets the highest profit. Those who succeed make profit and then expand their coast. In the same fashion, those who don't satisfy, fail loose profit and surely must contrast. The best always occupy the top position in a free enterprise/free market system.

At one time African had to import all of her steel and the bye products. Now there are steel production plants across the continent and with the completion of Ajaokuta Steel Plant in Nigeria joining it will even strengthen the steel industry the more—while the steel industry of the develop nations' is falling apart and facing stiffed competition from other second world countries. Years ago all of petroleum oil and gas industry was controlled by the developed nations, to us it was all strange. But today, the future of the industry belongs to Africa—a fact even the civilized nations humbly agree to.

Road networks around the continent were only imagined, but now the transport industry is one of the largest industries in Africa. Both by rail, road and air. There are over 4000 airports across the continent with her aviation industry has one of the largest.

Some of the largest industries in the west and some of the biggest companies in America are now broke and in Financial ruin. The growth industries of those countries are in trouble waters today. That is to say, things that were of good choice yesterday could be of no option today.

Times change, so does taste process and styles. The competent individual with a brilliant new idea cause positive change: so consumers change options; the consumers rush for the newest, brandest idea.

The free market is so complex with all sorts of competition and the more complex and uncertain it is, the more better chance any individual has to recognize an opportunity in the form of a product or service or some combination of the two as a need the consuming public desires to be satisfied—and are willing to pay for it.

Looking at it critically, the more complex the society becomes the more difficult it will be for centralized government to control and direct the affairs of the individual public. The free enterprise system is no doubt the best way to decentralize the government both for the consumer and the competing producers. Today's entrepreneur is very lucky to live in this age of an advanced society with its bundles of opportunities.

It is easier for Africans to build multi-national corporations today than it ever was. It requires as much effort in the 1900's to build an enterprise than to build five enterprises today.

In a world's economy dominated by giant western corporations it will be inspiring to observe the supersonic movement of free trade repeatedly knock down inefficient large-scale operations and are overtaken by up and coming business from third-world countries who are out—performing the world' leaders. The standard for effectiveness and efficiency with changing times gives all the advantage to new corporations or individuals who have insight and vision to recognized and grab opportunities with passion, determination, diligence and courage to act.

While the large western multinational lack flexibility, the single visionary individuals have it. All of this large multinationals are run by managers who are salaried and responsible for large budgets, that makes them very careful and routinely and sluggish still in their movement. These managers are less likely to identify small risky opportunities with minor profit that would averagely have increased the net turnover. But the smart, agile enthusiastic new, small—scale entrepreneur can make a major financial break by nose—diving on the same opportunity. That is why they say it is easier to climb to the top than to remain at the top. Little by little, this new individual or company begins to build her vast business and financial empire.

Now we hear of African telecom multinational like Vodacom, MTN, V-Mobile, and Globacom who have broken the monopoly of giant western Telecom companies. We hear of cars, computers and other jet age technologies are also manufactured here in Africa.

Bishop David Oyedepo's winners chapel's Faith Tabernacle is the world's largest single church auditorium, located at Canaan land Ota Nigeria. The ministry itself has an array of business networks spread all over the continent of Africa, Europe and America including a world-class university right there at Ota.

Business are rising everyday people are changing the face of business in this continent. People like Aliko Dangote, Mike Adenuga, Wale Tinubu, Pascal Dozie just to mention but a few who are employers of labor to its thousands.

What about the African Americans who are at the thick of all the actions outside there—people like Oprah Winfrey, who recently hit a one billion dollar net worth as the highest earning woman. The likes of M.D. Ben Carson who was the youngest neuro-surgeon at the age of 33 and head of neuro-surgery department at John Hopkins one of the world's biggest hospital. T.D Jakes that Dallas preacher is the CEO of about three national corporations in America. Myles Munroe (Dr) from the Bahamas is a consultant to over nine different governments and numerous corporations including Sony Corporation and Microsoft—of course he is telling them what to do to get the good results they desire. I won't forget the Nigerian Philip Enegwana, that computer guru who recently developed a computer that can solve 1 billion mathematical questions in one minute—of course that's the fastest computer machine and he said he wants them to be used in weather forecasting and oil exploration. And then Michael Jordan—a recent gull-up poll showed that Jordan's face was the most known face on planet earth. His face is known more than that of any world's leader and could be easily recognized by even kid in Singapore, Malawi, Cape-Verde and very tiny Islands.

What will happen to this continent if only part of their glory could bring a new dimension to the situation back home.

Talent and a good idea turn opportunity into fortune. The real question is how to identify your gift and talent and what to do with it once you've identified it. That small seed inside of you is a seed of fortune once properly nurtured. Only the simple realistic visioner with an appetite for goal and growth will be able to nurture that little seed into a full size tree—and who knows a forest.

Asa Candler, a back woods Georgia drug Clerk, gave his life savings to a country doctor who was holding a charred black kettle of viscous ooze and a slip of paper containing the syrup's formula. Asa Candler transformed his five hundred dollars investment into a soft drink that came to be named Coca-Cola.

The skillful entrepreneur can turn almost any circumstance into a seed for growing financial fortune. Honda motors started out in a Tokyo garage, Hilton Hotels started with five rooms in the family compound house, Roy Krock Mc Donald started as one drive—in restaurant, general electric started as Edison's laboratory, Wall-mart, chick—A—fils, Kentucky chicken, Mary K—Cosmetics all started small. God first created one man and the two, three, four and at one time there were fifty people on the surface of the earth and at another time five hundred, five million and six billion today. Every thing big started small.

How did all these business differ from the rest—what they did was, they took a good idea and coupled it with a plan. They had a firmly defined goal they were after, and were motivated to implement their plan through hard work. They invested and re-invested, using the laws of geometric progression and compounding interest to compound their investment over and over again. First they all started with one shop, plant, factory, employee or one product. Then there were two, soon four, eight, sixteen, thirty—two, sixty-four and on and on in that manner.

If this folks can do it, why can't you do it as well? These things can happen to anybody and it can happen any where!

AH! ALL YOUNG PEOPLE HEAR THIS

—STRATEGIC INVESTMENT—

Strategy simply refers to the working of the mind. It implies thinking, reasoning and planning through any of life's circumstances seen or unforeseen. Strategic investment therefore means the formation of a plan and the process of operation so as to secure a future return in your life as concerning your faith, your family and your finances.

As we are growing up, our role models are not limited to some examples at home, school community or church.

Neither are only historic or Biblical heroes. All of the society—including literature, entertainment, and media—highlighted and celebrated the lives and stories of money such individuals worthy of emulation. The setting was the same in so many movies I have watched on Television even as a Kid—the trials and adventures of admirable people who worked and fought and struggled until they emerged victories over whatever circumstances that challenged them.

I have watched and liked movies Mel Gibson's 'Brave Heart and 'Patriots'. This setting as been the same repeatedly—whether it be historic tales about pioneers braving the frontiers, migrants arriving on a new place with nothing but a dream and the clothes on their backs, orphans growing up to become giant entrepreneurs and industrialists, outnumbered soldiers somehow and by someway accomplishing their mission. Many such movies were based on true life's stories. though there are lots of inclusion making them look unrealistic, but the spirit they embodied and the massage they instilled both reflect and shape a real societal belief in the positive power of such character traits as determination, integrity, intelligence, courage, faith and a willingness to work to succeed against all odd.

Well this might not be a great place to start telling the inspiring true stories of the remarkable people our world has today. But quickly we can take some antidotes from T.D. Jakes.

For one who has a young family man faced frailty, he said of those times, "our financials were incredibly weak, and my faith in myself and in God was definitely on trail." Only T.D. Jakes and a few friends remember how they struggled and fought their way up after their factory got burnt completely and closed. How they survived unemployment, applied for welfare for a brief period, and had their car reposed. He said, "We lost everything but our faith, which paid off in spades! My wife had to boil bathing water for me on an electric range when the gas was disconnected. She created meals from nothing and never once complained. She dressed the bleeding hands I had from digging ditches and lifted my bruised ego the first time I had to go get milk from the WIK program. It is from our life together that I extract the nuggets of wisdom that will hopefully empower others to run on broken legs, crawl on crushed knees, and stand on twisted feet. Together we have survived through the winds of life, burying our parents, raising our children, endearing the plights and plagues of being human while expected to be divine. It has not been easy."

These nuggets of wisdom are contained in his book, 'the great investment'. T.D Jakes has something to say to all the young people out there who aspire for greatness in this journey of life—I think it's a must read.

'THE GREAT INVESTMENT'

Yes, all of life is an investment. Where there is a great investment, there will be great return. Where there is little investment, there is little return. Life doesn't afford us the opportunity to pay what we like and still gain what we want. We need to invest today, so that we can reap the reward tomorrow. We must be like the ants and prepare for tomorrow today. I know a lot of people who failed to be the ants and in the winter of their lives were depressed and resentful, cursing their wasted youth. They didn't invest in the future and later in life found themselves in a financial, emotional and spiritual state of poverty. They died poor, bitter and complaining for lack of an invested life's plan.

"GO TO THE ANT, YOU SLUGGARD, CONSIDSER ITS WAYS AND BE WISE! IT HAS NO COMMANDER, NO OVERSEER OR RULER, YET IT STORES ITS PROVISION IN SUMMER AND GATHERS ITS FOOD AT HARVEST. HOW LONG WILL YOU LIE THERE, YOU SLUGGARD? WHEN WILL YOU GET UP FROM YOUR SLEEP? A LITTLE SLEEP, A LITTLE SLUMBER A LITLLE FOLDING OF THE HANDS TO REST AND POVERTY WILL COME ON YOU LIKE A BANDIT AND SCARCITY LIKE AN ARMED MAN"

—Proverb 6:6-11

The ants are preparing, the birds are building there nests, the beaver is constructing his dam. All of creation invest in the future, prepares for the winter, and delay gratification for the purpose of a better tomorrow. We should follow their lead and begin to set our sights on tomorrow while maximizing our movement today. We need to invest in the future.

Onward, fellow travelers! God speed! Take this humble offering, the sum of my life experience thus far. Use this advice to set a course for your future, formulate a strategy to carry it out and gain the strength and inspiration to see it through. Dare to dream and aim for goals far beyond your current position. Seek to move ahead and reach height un-imagined. Keep your sights set on the future and be ever mindful of the legacy you leave behind.

One thing is certain: you have a day to be born and a day to die, and in between you have the greatest investment you will ever make. You invest your time, your strength, your youth, and ultimately, like Christ, you are laying your life down in your business, in your relationships, in your church. Every day that passes is a day spent a day you will never see again. You cannot stop the spending process. But you can control where you spend your days, with whom you spend them, and what you spend them on. You want the most beneficial return on every day spent, don't you? Then make the great investment—in your faith, family—and finance—and have the time of your life!

Honestly, my heart goes for all aspiring people out there. I'm repeating it as I said it earlier on—stop the madness! Invest in your future because there is always something to do, to get the result you desire. What is that in your hands? Your gift, your talents, your money, you time, your strength, your youthfulness, your spirit, your body, your emotions, and your mind. Invest them. Put them in things that will appreciate with time and not depreciate. The way you make you bed is the way you'll lay on it. Don't forget. I know that the God of heaven will never let you down. Amen!

HAND OFF—UNCLE SHEGE

As voters, we need to become personally involved and elect officials who will dedicate themselves to getting and keeping the government out of business and encourage more business people to get into government. One look at NEPA, NITEL, Refineries, government hospitals government school and all the poverty alleviation programs will convince any one that despite the efforts of tens of thousands of dedicated government employees, who have devoted a chunk of their lives to conscientiously serving Nigeria and the general public, the government simply doesn't know how to run a business.

The need for more direction and encouragement in business principles are painfully evident when we view the rising cost of government and its comparative inefficiencies. For example, OANDO can ship barrels of petrol from the United State to Nigeria faster and cheaper than it will take any of the government refineries to refine one gallon of petrol. Incidentally, the government can only provide as many services (like the refineries and others) as productive people and profitable businesses can support.

Some couples of years back, you could make a telephone call from Nigeria to New York for three hundred naira or you could mail several letters before one eventually arrives. To day you can call New York at any time of the day for twenty naira and with the E-mail, you could mail a letter there and then; and get a report if it has been delivered.

If it were government that were running Cybar Cafes, it would have been nothing to write home about. Of even more concern is a recent survey which shows that the rate of productivity per man hour in government is thirty—nine percent below the average productivity level of the private sector.

Thirty—nine percent! No wonder our national budget runs into red by the billions years after years.

Howbeit, as concerned citizens we need to show case the progress instead of the problems. I don't believe in hiding problems, but I believe the best way to solve a problem is to identify it. Then we need to remember that hope and encouragement are the major ingredient in the solution to any problem. We also need to remember that some good comes out of every problem. The prophets of doom assured us at one time that the increasing size of the population was going to make farm land very scarce, our children will grow up in an era of darkness and education would be destroyed. Then some one discovered petroleum on our land.

Between now and the time you read this words there could well be a dozen national emergencies and numbers of crises in your personal life. However, always remember that the only people who don't have problems are those in the cemeteries. And even some of them really have problems. If you have problems—personal or national—it simply means you are alive and the more problems you have the more alive you are. With humor I will suggest that if you don't have man—sized problems you should get on your knees and ask God to 'trust' you with a few.

RESOURCES AND RESOURCEFULNESS

National dedication will enable us to utilize our greatest natural resources—our people—who will then develop our other resources which Nigeria have in abundance. This includes the discovered and undiscovered, the known and the unknown. I agree with anyone who says "our major problem is not a lack of resources but a lack of resourcefulness".

Our oil reserves might be running low but our hidden resources will more than take up the slack. Just about 50 years ago people were using coal as fuel. Just over thirty years ago, Africa has not known the use of uranium.

Unfortunately, we are not utilizing many of our known natural resources. Over approximately the next twenty years, "natural gas is projected to be the fastest growing primary energy source worldwide," states the international energy out look 2003 report (IEO 2003 report). Natural gas is the cleanest burning of the fossil fuels, and it is thought that Nigeria holds vast reserves of natural gas. However, "no one really knows exactly how much natural gas exits until it is extracted", states the Washington D.C. based natural gas supply association. "Each estimate is based on a different set of assumptions............it thus difficult to get a definitive answer to the question of how much natural gas exits.

Yes, it will have an increased methane emission, but modern technology is on the threshold of removing and utilizing that methane greenhouse gas. One state in the Niger Delta only has enough natural gas reserves to supply more energy than all known oil reserves in the entire country. In short, here's a "lemon" I'm confident will end up as the principle ingredient in lemonade.

Solar heat, wind and atomic energy are being developed daily and some experts feel that with a concerted effort, these could provide a major part of our home and office heating supply in the very near future. Tremendous potential also exist in the development of offshore drilling. I'm not definite about the percentage of our waters that has been leased for oil exploration and drilling thus far, but maybe not up to 25%. The list of undeveloped resources is endless especially if we go into agriculture, steel, solid minerals etc. I'm confident that Nigerian's ingenuity will solve the energy problem as well as any other problem we are positive about solving.

IN LOVE WITH AMERICA

For many, America is definitely that country that they love to hate. But even in conflicts of opinions, we must cooperate with them because we need America's aid. We can't afford to run the risk of having conflicts with America. The truth is American and Nigerian are both "essentially democratic and Individualistic" and so the two countries can complement each other economically.

The next time you visit America, board a jet and do a little sight-seeing as you fly up the coast. Look down on the forest of giant sequoias and Redwoods before you turn right and cross the awe inspiring Rockies. Now you get a bird's eye-view of the corn and wheat fields of Kansas, Nebraska and Illinois which has helped make America the bread basket of the world. you fly over Chicago, the home of a former newspaper boy named clement stone, a free enterpriser who conceived a better idea to merchandise insurance and built a personal fortune, still rated at roughly half of a billion dollars, despite the fact that he has contributed over 500 million dollars to worthwhile courses. Today Mr. stone shares his success secret through his books, tapes, recordings and monthly publications like "success unlimited".

Continuing your trip, you turn northeast across Lake Michigan and in a matter of minutes come to Ada, Michigan, the home of Rich De Vos and Jay Van Andel, two of the most successful and vocal exponents of the free enterprise system in America today. There belief in the system is founded on personal experience. In 1957, they acquired a converted service station and started Amway, which is a contraction of the 'American way.' Their capital was limited and their problems were numerous, but an unlimited faith in God and country combined with an enormous, capacity for work, prevailed. Today the Amway corporation distributes it's product through approximately 2 million independent distributors worldwide, who themselves sold over two billion dollars in 1996 in Canada, Germany, England, France, Hong Kong, Australia and the United States. As a matter of fact, just some couple of years after the company started in that converted service station; we can say with poetic accuracy that the sun never sets on an Amway Distributor.

Less I forget, did I give you the story of Richard Cessna, Jr.? He is the president of Kidco, Inc. which has been in business for sometime now, but they are already millionaires. The started with a contract to sweep the six main streets of San Deigo country Estates for 150 dollars per month. They branched out to contracting with their father, the supervisor of the estates' 110 horse stables, to remove the manure and wood shavings which they compost. They sell the compost to landscapers and local golf courses at prices lower than commercial suppliers. Incidentally, Richard Cessna, Jr. is 12 years old. His vice president is his sister, age 9. the secretary of the company is another sister, age 11, and the treasurer is a half sister who is 14. Now that is America for you. That is free enterprise at work.

I HEARD THOSE WORDS.

Following the certification of his November, 2004 victory at the United States presidential polls, president George W. Bush was inaugurated January this year for a second term and pledged a sweeping spread of liberty and freedom. In a speech considered as one of the greatest in the history of America, among others, he said this word:......"For as long as whole regions of the world simmer in resentment and tyranny, prone to ideologies that feed hatred and feed murder, violence will gather and multiply in destructive power and cross the most defended borders and raise a mortal threat.

There is only one force of history that can break the reign of hatred and resentment and expose the pretension of tyranny and reward the hopes of the decent and tolerant, and that is the force of human freedom.

America's vital interests and our deepest belief are now one. From the day of our founding, we have proclaimed that every man and woman on this earth has rights and dignity and matchless value, because they bear the image of the maker of heaven and earth.

Across the generations, we have proclaimed the imperative of self government, because no one is fit to be a master and no one deserves to be a slave. Freedom by it's nature, must be chosen and defended by citizens and sustained by the rule of law and the protection of minorities.

We will persistently clarify the choice before every ruler and every nation. The moral choice between oppression, which is always wrong and freedom which is eternally right.

In the long run, there is no justice without freedom, and there can be no human right without human liberty—the ruler of outlaw regime can know that we still believe as Abraham Lincoln did: "those who deny freedom to others deserve it not for themselves, and, under the rule of a just God, cannot long retain it."

The leaders of government with long habits of control need to know: to serve your people you must learn to trust them. Start on this journey of progress and justice and America will stand at your side.

By our effort we have lit a fire as well: a fire in the mind of men. It warms those who feel its power. It burns those who fight its progress. And one day this untamed fire of freedom will reach the darkest corners of the world.

I ask our youngest citizens to believe the evidence of your eyes. You have seen duty and allegiance in the determined faces of our soldiers. You have seen that life is fragile, and evil is real, and courage triumphs.

Make a choice to serve in a cause that is larger than your wants, larger than yourself, and in your days you will add not just to the wealth of our country, but to it's character.

America has need of idealism and courage, because we have essential work at home: the unfinished work of American freedom. In a world moving towards liberty, we are determined to show the meaning and promise of liberty.

In America's ideal for freedom, citizens find the dignity and security of economic independence, instead of laboring on the edge of subsistence.

This is the broader definition of liberty that motivated the Homestead Act, the social security Act and the G.I. Bill of rights.

And now we will extend this vision by reforming great institutions to serve the need of our time.

To give every American a stake in the promise and future of our country, we will bring the highest standards to our schools and build an ownership society.

We will widen the ownership of homes and businesses, retirement savings and health insurance, preparing our people for the challenges of life in a free society.

By making every citizen an agent of his or her own destiny, we will give our fellow Americans greater freedom, from want and fear and make the society more prosperous and just and equal.

In America's ideal for freedom, the public interest depends on private character, on integrity, and tolerance towards others, and the rule of conscience in our own lives.

Self-government relies, in the end, on the governing of the self. That edifice character is build in families, supported by communities with standards, and sustained in our national life by the truth of Sinia, the sermon on the mount, the words of the Koran, and the varied faith of our people.

Americans move forward in every generation by reaffirming all that is good and true that come before: ideals of justice and conduct that are the same yesterday, today and forever.

In America's ideal of freedom, the exercise of rights is ennobled by service and mercy and a heart for the weak.
Liberty for all does not mean independence from one another. Our nation relies on men and women who look after a neighbour and surrounds the lost with love.

Americans at our best values of life we se in one another and must always remember that even the unwanted have worth.

From the perspective of a single day, including this day of dedication, the issues and questions before our country are many.

From the viewpoint of centuries, the questions that came to us are narrowed and few. Did our generation advance the cause of freedom? And did our character bring credit to that?

These questions that judge us also unit us, because Americans of every party and background, Americans by choice or by birth, and bound to one another in the cause of freedom.

We have known divisions, which must be healed to move forward in great purposes. And I will strive in good faith to heal them. Yet hose divisions do not define America.

We felt the unity and fellowship of our nation when freedom came under attack, and our response came like a single hand over a single heart.

And we can feel that same unity and pride whenever America acts for good, and the victim of disaster are given hope, and the unjust encounter justice, and the captives are set free.

We go forward with complete confidence in the eventual triumph of freedom. Not because history runs on the wheels of inevitability: it is human choices that move events. Not because we consider ourselves a chosen nation; God moves and chooses as he wills.

We have confidence because freedom is a permanent hope of mankind, the hunger in dark places, the longing of the soul.

When our founders declared a new order of the ages, when soldiers died in wave upon wave for a union based on liberty, when citizens marched in peaceful outrage under the banner "Freedom Now" they were acting on the ancient hope that is meant to be fulfilled.

History has an ebb and flow of justice, but history also has a visible direction, set by liberty and the author of liberty.

When the declaration of independence was first read in public and the liberty bell was sounded in celebration, a witness said "It rang as if it meant something" in our time it means something still.

America in this young century, proclaims liberty throughout all the world and to all the inhabitants thereof.

Renewed in our strength, tested but not weary, we are ready for the greatest achievement in the history of freedom.

May God bless you and may He watch over the United States of America.

—Excepts from President Bush's inauguration speech delivered on the west side of the U.S capitol in Washington D.C. Bush launched his second term with an argent pledge to spread freedom, a vow to heal divisions and a commitment to the ideal of freedom which is a free enterprise, and economic independence.

WE MUST SELL FREE ENTERPRISE TO EVERYBODY.

I could tell you a thousand other stories about people who prove the free enterprise system is the most effective economic system ever devised by man. It's a system that works so effectively that Americans relief recipient are in the upper 8% of the income brackets of the world. This means that over 4 billion people on the face of this earth aren't living as well as the relief recipient live in America.

Despite all the advantages of the free enterprise system, the most serious mistake we can make is to assume too much. We erroneously assume that we don't have to sell children, youths and fellow citizens on the obvious advantages and benefits associated with Africa and the free enterprise system. Results have been disturbing and disappointing to say the least. This attitude has bred revolt, rebellion, discord and such acts and comments that would have our founding fathers turning in their graves.

It has become crystal clear, therefore, that we do have to sell Africa and the free enterprise system to our children, because only one generation stands between us and all the other, disappointing economic and political system in the world. It's equally clear that we need to sell the free enterprise system to those teachers and professors who often belittle the very system that will sustain them. We need to sell labour leaders and union members on the concept that a labourer should be free to work as hard and as enthusiastically as he wishes for the benefit of everyone. That is free enterprise. That is what Africans should embrace fully.

We need to tell more of our citizens—some of whom are theoretically responsible—that their screaming about our "problems" is slowing down the steady route to the very system that will make us one of the most productive and affluent land on earth.

We also need to sell government employees and officials on the fact that government doesn't produce income or prosperity. Instead, it exists and survives because free people working in a free land support the government. We need to sell elected leaders on the simple fact that the right to work and produce without undue government restraint is not only our right but our source of strength. One good look at any "planned economy" or even still "mixed economy" will convince any clear thinker that free enterprise is the only way to go.

AFRICA IS IN YOUR HANDS

If I sound like a sentimentalist who is in love with Africa, I plead guilty—but with cause. When I look around, I hardly find any other continent or group of people that is like Africa. We're a people that is so blessed with human and natural resources more than any other part of the world. Foreigners rushing to come and get glimpse of some of nature's most outstanding beauty. We hardly hear of typhoons, hurricanes, earthquakes and the likes. Our lands are one of the best for Agriculture and farming. Africa my Africa, Africa of great warriors in harvestern Savannahs Africa of which my grand—mother always sings of Africa Oh Africa.

In my mind, there is absolutely no doubt that Africa is still the land of the free, still the home of the brave, still the land where anyone can get any thing he really wants—provided he is willing to take the necessary steps. Yes—I'm completely convinced that though our land is not perfect; it is far ahead of so many other lands on the face of the earth with its multitude of opportunities. It is truly Africa the beautiful and it is time that every loyal African starts standing up and speaking up for the land because this our generation is truly the last hope for freedom in Africa.

As Africans we have a tremendous land with absolutely unlimited opportunities accompanied by equally awesome responsibilities. This generation is the last, the one and the only hope that a dwindling free Africa has. Freedom like health is often appreciated only after we no longer have it. Historically, freedom, once lost is difficult to regain. According to freedom house, a nonpartisan organization devoted to the strengthening of free society, at the start of this new century, only 18.9% of African's population was free. This figure is down from 32% in the last two decades. You and I could just be all that stands between that 18.9% and slavery.

The United Nations either can't or won't do any thing to help protect the free people of Africa. Since its inception over half a billion people have lost their freedom in Africa alone. In short, the U.N has fallen short of its function as a positive factor for peace and is little more than a pawn of the big league countries. Its ineptness in enforcing peace in Rwanda, Congo DR, Burundi, Liberia, Sierra lone, Somalia, Uganda, Coted'viore and a dozen other places. Including its refusal to act in the face of undeniable proof that the Sudanese government is deliberately killing its citizens in Danfur, should clearly prove that the U.N either cannot or will not function.

The voting structure of the U.N, combined with the fact that since its inception no African country has been given a permanent seat in the Security Council, renders the U.N a little ineffective as an unbiased body for world peace.

With the big league nations in control of that body, as one expert rightly points out in "voice of Africa", "it's like asking the fox to guard the henhouse and we are the chickens".

One reason I wrote this book and created "success way inc." entrepreneur-ship development program—in molding African entrepreneur is to help alert Africa to the greatest crises in our long history and to help build our strength by building our people. I wanted to be able to at any time look my children and your children in the eye and say I did my part and then some in fighting the battle to insure each of you the same opportunity for the good life which God so generously bestows on us. Its true as I said earlier, this generation is the last hope of Africa to free and separate her from all the bad economic systems and governance it has suffered all this far. Dorothy Thompson says, "no one can have life, liberty or the possibility of happiness unless his country is alive, free and happy".

What about you? Are you accepting your responsibility? If everyone in Africa was doing exactly the same thing you're doing, would our country be getting better, or worse? That's a question for you and your conscience. If you really love Africa, you will enthusiastically join the ever-increasing throng working to make a great Africa even greater.

BITS AND PIECES

In this concluding part, I give you bit and pieces, for you to select those you need in your life and to link the dots to a glorious future. Enjoy it.

- Every great business enterprise and institution you see today began with a dream.

- Thought are things; and powerful thing at that especially when mixed with faith and definiteness of purpose.

- More gold had been mined from the thoughts of men than has ever been taken from the earth.

- We are the master of our fate, the captain of our soul because we have the power of choice.

- Always maintain a spirit of open mindedness.

- Dreams come true when desire transforms them into concrete action.

- You too can form a business enterprise—
  To pursue a legal and profitable business interest to the benefit of your associates, stake holders and the general public.

- All achievements, all earned riches, have their beginning in an idea.

- What you don't earn does not enhance your worth.

- Everyone needs a brother to help him/her establish his/her dream except for those who don't have dreams.

- To live without a dream is to be doomed

- Living without a goal is what makes one a scapegoat.

- A dream is the foundation for any meaningful break-through in life.

- The point is we must make ourselves relevant to our world

- You should be able to build businesses that will prosper and become a powerful force in YOUR COUNTRY and beyond, employing a strong labour force and making effective use of our resources.

- To make maximum impact, your initial financial and physical investments are put into worthy ideas which make you a producer and translate you to a front runner. Be flexible.

- Pay the initial price—that's all. It is essential to give before you get. Great men had to this before practical business could be turned into businesses that works for the public.

- With God in partnership with you, your business is secured. I always encourage people to give a part of their personal profit to God—through donations to churches, the poor and the needies, charity homes and missionary work.

- Opportunities abound everywhere.

- Money makes money. Let money work for you.

- The distance between success and mediocrity is due to three forces information, motivation, and association.

- Knowledge is power, influence, money, knowledge is worth everything it may cost you to obtain it.

- Stay focused with a long—term view, to learn to think about life—be a nerd (if your eye be single your body will be full of light)

- Use your brain to plan and prepare for the future.

- Don't go from day to day responding to circumstances rather create different ones

- Think about the future—set goals develop a deliberate plan to get there in grand style

- You have the capacity to determine the direction of your life; what you do with this potential will largely depend on there factors: your priorities, your principle, and your choices.

- Separate daily demands and real priorities

- Be careful to define what really interest and satisfies you with your highest priorities

- Always compensate the people around you who are effected by the pursue of your dreams for those extra labour and time they put in

- You must give something back as a positive impact on the society as a whole.

- The major principle to establish any great dream are discipline, hard work, teamwork

- Association is not by force, but by choice.

- Avoid instance gratification of the lifestyle for the rich and famous you see on television.

- - Every dream and lifestyle that directs you life should grew out of a relationship with God—make it a daily habit of prayer and bible reading.

- SEX—don't use condoms, use conduct

- Instead of begging anyone for financial aid, you could put the same amount of initiative, thought, and time into devising a strategy for achieving your goals yourself than in trying to get some rich and famous to help you. I guest you'll be a lot further along in the game.

- Stop looking for excesses and explanations for why things are the way they are, look for solutions—you are an overcome.

- Your adviser's assessment of your intelligence and potential might be wrong

- You can analyze the reasons for your failures and come up with a workable strategy for solving any problem.

- The real issue is not whether you can learn, work, and keep, a relationship—but how!

- To overcome hardship, you must look for role models who did overcome and work at being a positive example to the people around you.

- Set your sight high, stick to them, and work at it very, very hard. Invest in others and allow people invest in you.

- It is far more satisfying to talk your way out of trouble than to handle it physically.

- Many kids need scholarship to the university in Africa. Give them if you have.

- Reach for the stars decide what you want to be and don't settle for anything less

- Believe that you can live your dream, an then work toward that goal, and it will happen. The worst mistake you can make is when you give up on yourself.

- By reading, you can go anywhere, you would be anything you could imagine yourself out of a slum.

Walters seven rules to live

1. Know who is responsible—"I am responsible" when you begin with these three words, you can build a new life, even a new world.

2. Believe in some thing big—when we commit to high idea, we succeed before the out come is known. Your life is worth a noble motive.

3. Practice tolerance—you'll like yourself a lot and so will others.

4. Be brave—remember, courage is acting with fear, not without it. If the challenge is important to you, you are supposed to be nervous; we only worry about things we care about.

5. Love some one—because you should know joy.

6. Be ambitious—No single effort will solve all of your problem, achieve all of your dreams, or even be enough—and that is okay to want to be more than we are is real and normal and healthy.

7. Smile—because no one else can do this for you.

- Wisdom Principle:—the proof of desire is pursuit!

- You will always struggle, subconsciously to become the self-portrait you believe you're self to be.

- The day you make a decision about your life is the day your world will change.

- Accept responsibility for your financial future.

- The gifts God has given you are enough to bring you before great men.

- Jealousy over others' success kills your own creativity and dampens your influence.

- A budget can bring focus to your financial affairs.

- Know were your money is going; keep accurate records of all spending.

- Always expect, ask for, and get a receipt.

- A budget is not to restrict you from enjoying life, but it is a tool to help you focus your finances on those goals that will allow you to lead a fulfilling life.

- Then learn to distinguish between your need and your wants.

- You don't excel in any thing except you are committed to excellence in it.

- If you must be successful in business and life in general, you must contact Networking.

- You should produce something with your own trade mark and be able to sell your products to the market.

- You don't need to look for cheap money, cheap money murders destiny.

- There is already an industrial revolution springing up in Nigeria and you should be among the front runner that are making things happen and not a mere spectator.

- Christianity is not an escape flight to heaven but a design to make you influence the world for God.

- You are the hope of Africa.

- It is time to wake up—take your destiny in your hand and grab the unlimited opportunity.

- What you need is common sense not copper cent.

- One of the main weaknesses of mankind is the average man's familiarity with the word 'impossible'

- No irresponsible man has a future—responsibility is the price to greatness

- No one is born to greatness, some just go out there day after day and lay claim to it. Because the perpetual quest for perfection is something fate respects.

- Nothing you have imagined will work unless you do. The Bible, a book of faith, talks about work over 500 times.

- Often, the simple answer to a happy life and success is 'do'.

- Be a doer and not a hearer or sayer only deceiving yourself.

Tackling the barriers to successful planning

1. Fear of change

2. Ignorance

3. Uncertainty about the future

4. Lack of imaginations

Prayers; O' Lord,

- Help us to move beyond the idea of mediocrity in terms of job security because some of us may never need to work for any government or company but build our own and create our world of financial freedom.

- Help us to make deep career and business changes in our lives.

- Help us to move with the information age.

- Aid us in choosing new options, new directions and new financial future.

- "You cannot teach a person anything; you can only help him find it within himself"—Galileo. So we must discover the talents within our self and change our society positively.

- Build courage and creativity in us to take calculated risk which is the essential of an entrepreneur.

- Many people will not head down the street until all the lights are green. That is why they don't go anywhere!

- Formulate for us a road map to our all-round success.

- Help us to help each individual turn his dream of independence into reality

- Help us to inspire noble deeds.

- To help us set goals and achieve them.

- To smoothen our relationship with our creator

  "Success is everything"

"O' Lord we have no strength o wisdom of our own to face this great challenge that is before us neither do we even know what to do, but our eyes are on you—to lead, direct, protect and give us your wisdom and grace. We are depending on you Lord, to take control of our lives, families and businesses because anything put in your hand is safe. So help us God! Amen!

BACK PAGE

REFERENCE AND RECOMMENDED READING LIST

1. "Compassionate Capitalism" by Rich Devos
2. The burden of freedom" by Myles Munroe
3. "The big picture" by M.D. Ben Carson
4. "Steps to the top" by Zig Ziglar
5. "Sign post on the road to success" by E.W Keyon
6. "How to achieve total Success" by Russ Von Hoelscher
7. "Secret of the Millionaires" By George Sterne
8. "How to think like a millionaire" by Charles-Albert Poissant
9. "The great Investment: Faith, family and finance" by T.D. Jakes.
10. "The trouble with Nigeria" by Chinua Achebe
11. "Wealth of Nations" by Adam Smith
12. "See you at the top" by Zig Ziglar
13. "Success Digest Magazine"
14. "The Economist" Magazine

Other Selected Bibliography

1. Kroc, Ray and Anderson, Robert, 'Grinding it out: The making of McDonalds (Henry Regney, 1977).
2. Ford, Henry, 'My life and Work' (Doubleday, 1926)

3. Conrad Hilton: 'Be my guest'

4. John D. Rockefeller. 'Memoirs'

5. Thomas Kuhn "The Structure of Scientific Revolution"

*Nigeria and Indonesia: The political Economy of poverty, equity and growth," by David L. Bevan, Paul Collier and Jan Willem Gunning. Oxford University Press, 1999.

978-0-595-40383-7
0-595-40383-2

www.ingramcontent.com/pod-product-compliance
Lightning Source LLC
Chambersburg PA
CBHW030309290526
45785CB00001B/273